REPORT ON JUVENILE DELINQUENCY

MASS OBSERVATION

REPORT ON JUVENILE
DELINQUENCY

by

H. D. Willcock

faber and faber

This edition first published in 2009
by Faber and Faber Ltd
Bloomsbury House, 74–77 Great Russell Street
London WC1B 3DA

Printed by CPI Antony Rowe, Eastbourne

A CIP record for this book is available from the British Library

ISBN 978–0–571–25146–9

CONTENTS

INTRODUCTION

by Tom Harrison

My friend, Robin Maugham, who encouraged us to make this small survey, has prevailed upon me to write an introductory note. Since I was one of the originators of Mass-Observation back in 1937, and I am still actively associated with it, any additional words from me might appear redundant. But in the case of the present report, I have had little enough to do with it directly. The greater part of the work has fallen on Mass-Observation's field investigation staff, with especial spare-time help from Mr. Ivan Piercy, a young conscientious objector, who was himself imprisoned with juvenile criminals (because he refused to accept a medical examination for the Forces). Mass-Observation also had invaluable voluntary assistance from others, notably the Rev. D. B. Kittermaster and Mrs. F. Meichtrey, as well as some who are personally concerned—for instance, as officials or as criminals—with these problems, and cannot therefore be named here. The general burden of sorting out the vast mass of information collected and shaping it into this report has fallen upon my friend and colleague, H. D. Willcock.

A Report of this nature can only touch upon some of the problems, and in the space available here, Mass-Observation can indeed only touch upon a fraction of the material collected in this investigation alone. If the report that follows has a special value—and I venture to believe it has—it is in the semi-documentary presentation of a worm's eye view.

There is no attempt here to produce any new theory, or to generalise widely. This is a mild experiment in approach. In the

9

field of juvenile delinquency, and indeed of 'moral' problems in general, a new, non-partisan, 'deadpan' approach is overdue. In the past, even great experts and scholars in these fields have quickly been led into certain stereotype attitudes, or to over-specialise their interests, and narrow their points of view. From this small research we have learned much which we hope to apply in further and fuller investigations. And I hope that other interested persons may learn a little, too.

To me, the most important thing that emerges is the aimlessness, the drifting undertones in so much of 'modern youth'—if I may use that phrase without being unctuous. Not all of modern youth, by any means; far from that. And indeed, in a sense there is actual danger in the considerable proportion of modern young people who *are* citizen-conscious, alert, interested, well adjusted, intellectually alive, and if not spiritually satisfied, at least in active search of inspiration.

For the more educated, intellectual, important or better-off among older people (I write aged thirty-five years) tend to be too easily satisfied with what they see of our successors at the universities or in the youth organisations. It is so easy to forget other elements less conspicious.

Only when others gain the conspicuous limelight of the Courts or crime do we recognise them again. As such extreme young people are relatively few in number, they can easily be turned into a 'problem group' or written off as special, peculiar, misfit, maladjusted and so on. Moreover, the actions which society takes to deal with them as 'outsiders' can as readily be accepted by our far away and more 'respectable' eyes. All sorts of things can be going on behind the façade of legislative, administrative, on-paper and theoretical organisation, while sympathetic people point with pride to the façade itself as proof of our intelligent goodwill. Lately, the public conscience has been stirred by the Curtis Report on certain problems for young and homeless children; before this piece of research (which was stimulated by certain dramatic breakdowns and 'scandals') the great majority of serious citizens were satisfied that all was well on that front. Not long after came the Nuffield Report on Old People, which showed a deplorable state of affairs in

Institutions upon which Britain has often prided herself, and of which she has boasted abroad. I believe that an impartial and thorough report in the field of *every* type of unit dealing with the adolescent and the 'young person' would show at least an equally 'surprising' situation. It would be a much more difficult study to make, and many very powerful groups would be concerned, naturally and honourably enough, to make special efforts to put a good face on their parts of the affair. But in this Mass-Observation study we have already had something stronger than a whiff of really astonishing goings on. Some of the reports we have received, for instance, from a senior official about approved schools, from a warden in a famous prison, have been so extraordinary that we have preferred to wait, check and reserve judgement. We have omitted any type of sensationalism in the present account, and avoided any report with which we are not fully satisfied. Even so, our mild and minor activities have produced quite anxious enquiries from, for instance, the Prison Commissioners—a body, by the way, with immense responsibilities which have not always been sufficiently scrutinised by Parliament and the people.

Thus, dramatic undertones are present. A trace of them inevitably filters into even the coolest and most detached study of juvenile delinquency. But this report primarily seeks to set a wider canvass. Though Mass-Observation was asked specifically to study juvenile *delinquency*, approaching it without expertese or preconception, it soon became clear that juvenile delinquency was an inseparable part of the pattern of many other researches Mass-Observation have done and most other institutions that had been studied. This report is not the place to go into the whole of that. But I think the early sections will at least provide that atmosphere and suggest that approach, which, although not entirely novel, would I believe be found extremely fruitful in further studies—for instance, by psychiatrists, who have shown a commendable and increasing attention to this type of issue.

After all, let us face it. Who of us can truly say that in different times, with a different parental or income background—or even in the background and conditions that we had when aged

11

17—by some slight circumstances we might not have ended with the dishonourable title of Juvenile Delinquent. The unusual statistics of petty theft in the first sections of this report should be pondered by all of us. And perhaps any person who can thereafter feel wholly self-righteous is, in a way, more to be pitied than praised.

The other day I was giving a talk at Pentonville to an audience of some hundred of prisoners. In the early part of my talk, which was about parachuting, I asked them several questions, aimed to find people with interests or attitudes which I myself (as the speaker) held. I was almost literally staggered by the number there who held up their hands on these various points. There, I felt, but for the Grace of God, go I. Yet I do not think I have any less social sense than the next man, and I have spent a large part of my time attempting to do things which would be generally classed as constructive citizenship.

Is it not that the pattern of our civilisation is changing? We, closely bedded down in it, have the greatest difficulty in recognising all the changes. We see the changes in speed and technique, for they are indeed inescapably apparent—jet propulsion, atomic physics, plastic stockings. But the moral and mental changes are very hard to see. It is partly to meet this difficulty that Social Research and the Social Sciences generally have expanded with tremendous rapidity in the past decade. This is also why the need for their further expansion is immense. When we come to apply improved methods of Social Science to our civilisation as a whole, as we presently must, we shall see these things in a different light. We shall then be able to do more than merely isolate *individual* problems as they arise. At present this is necessary, owing to the lack of well-proven background social theory and the lack of sufficient research workers to cover the whole field. The social services are forced to cope with things as they become serious—war neuroses, crime, incentives in industry and so on.

I do not wish to over-generalise. But it seems to me clear that juvenile delinquency is only part of a much deeper and greater problem—the problem of uninspired and unadjusted youth. Kicking the bucket around or the endless intoxication of the slot machine in an Oxford Street Arcade, reflect something just as grave as breaking a window or pinching a watch. We have to deal with the one *ad hoc,* but we also have to deal with the other. It is indeed the key to the whole future of our way of life and the surviving health of our society. Those interested to pursue this line of thought will find it approached from different points of view in two recently published Mass-Observation studies, *Peace and the Public* (Longmans) and *Puzzled People* (Gollancz). I would only like to say personally here that I think Willcock's report, which follows, is not only intensely interesting to read as it stands, but interesting to think about as it reads. He has deliberately refrained from over-stating the case. For this is one of those cases which have so often been methodically, even dogmatically stated, with frequent contradictions. Understatement is, in this paradoxical sense, overdue. The reader has to do some of the *work* with the material that follows. Mass-Observation has not in the past been afraid of generalising, and there is plenty of it in the two books that I have referred to. In this case, the deadpan approach is, at present, the most suitable, I am convinced—or should I say convicted?

I

ONE YOUTH

From the Diary of a Prison Chaplain

14th May

Bill has been caught standing on the roof of the prison work-shop and removing his trousers so that he might expose himself to the ladies in the quarters opposite. He is in here for violent assault on girls. I propose to discuss his troubles with him thoroughly. His first sex experience was at fourteen, when he read a thriller in bed describing in detail the cutting of a woman's dead body by a murderer. This produced the first emission of his life, in him. Before that his mind had been full of sex images but he had had no sex experience. I have got so far and no farther than this.

22nd May

Some further talk with Bill. I tried to get him to talk of his home and childhood, but he was not very forthcoming. Switching to his present behaviour he talked more freely. He had not planned his original experiment in exhibitionism. He had been clearing out the gutters on the roof, and he had seen a woman's face in a window opposite. This had aroused his sex emotion, and he began to dwell on his former sex experience of violent assaults on women. After dinner he had climbed back on to the roof. Seeing a woman again at the window, he had openly masturbated, giving himself up at the same time to fantasies of violently assaulting the woman. His reactions after this first piece of exhibitionism were excitement, eagerness to do it again, no fear of consequence, a feeling that he ought to be ashamed. A curious and interesting fact is that his assaults on women took place in May and April last year, his exhibitionism during the same months this year.

23rd May

A short time only with Bill. He had written at my request last night an account of anything that came into his head after I had left him. He wrote a vivid description of a telegram arriving at his home announcing his father's death. I talked a little more about the exhibitionism to him, trying to persuade him that it was a sign of infantilism, that it was merely a relic of a common phenomenon of childhood . . . Anyhow, the lad is quite cheerful now. I have thought that he may have a great contempt for women in him, which would explain his desire to hurt them, and his exhibitionism to be a mark of contempt. He remembered, under examination, having read an account in the daily paper a year or two back of a man being arrested for exhibitionism. This left no conscious impression on his mind.

24th May

Further talk to Bill. After his first experience of masturbation at fourteen, he masturbated at not very frequent intervals. About the same time he began to keep company with a girl with whom he went out regularly until he was seventeen. He got a kick out of kissing her, but did not feel that he 'ought' to go any further. At the end of those three years she left the district. He was depressed in consequence. Going out one night he saw a girl, followed her on an impulse, with sex desire in his heart, came up behind her, put his hand over her mouth, pulled her over backwards, and ran away when she screamed. A few nights after he was on his way to the pit, saw another girl, followed her, hit her over the head with the pick handle, and when she screamed, ran away. A few nights later he followed yet another girl, pulled her over backwards, lay on the top of her, and began to put his hand up her clothes. She protested, and promised him money if he would desist. She gave him 3s. 10d., and he

16

made off. He cannot explain his violence. He only knows that on all three occasions he was miserable and ashamed of what he had done. There is evidently here a feeling of resentment against girls in general because he feels that they ought to be used for sex gratification, and yet he supposes that he ought not to use them because it is not 'right', and the consequent violent repression in him causes anger. He acknowledges that the affection for his mother is the great affection in his life, but I can find no trace of the mother complex which turns some men into homosexuals.

Passing from the story of these assaults to the story of his various exhibitionisms, he acknowledged that the main feeling in his mind when he exposed himself was one of anger against the woman in the window who 'tempted' him. His fantasies when masturbating are perfectly straightforward fantasies of naked women. There is no desire for violence. Nor any homosexual conflict.

25th May

Confined my attention to Bill to setting him a short poem to learn and asking him questions on it. This by way of an elementary lesson in concentration, mind control. He co-operated well and eagerly.

26th May

A short time only with Bill. Taught him a bit of concentration and mind control by getting him to count particular letters in a page of print. He says he feels perfectly happy in his mind now. And I think that it is true. I talked for a very short time to him on the stupidity of the ordinary ideas about sex, and dwelt on the fun and happiness of sex relationship of a girl and a man who loved each other and both wanted the fun and happiness with each other. But I do not think that I have yet removed the latent antagonism to women in his mind.

28th May

Had an hour and a half's talk with a psychologist in Harley

17

Street. He said some illuminating things about Bill 14th **May**. He said that he was probably an instance of a fracture between feeling and sensation. There had been a struggle of incompatibles going on in him. He has never been in love. He has somehow always been *at* loggerheads with life. Always *at,* never *in.* Always life got at him. He has retaliated by getting at life. He has so far been incapable of 'in', only capable of 'at'. He has wanted and got sensation. But what he really wanted and never got was feeling. It may be that he was born a Problem child, according to the pattern of his seed, incapable of affection. This I do not think is the case. But certainly when called upon to feel anything, he could not take it. Somewhere pain and harshness broke his heart. He set up in himself aggression against aggression. Life got at him, he got at life. Somehow he must be touched inside himself, so that he will in the end react to affection. Often such cases, said the Psychologist, will make you get at them, because this is the only way love speaks to them, for they have been got at themselves so long.

1st August

The unhappy Bill has broken out again. He attacked some girls in the woods. He is in a forgetful state to-night, right back in his old state of torment, wearing a tortured face. I saw him in the cells but could not help him in any way.

2nd August

I saw Bill off to the other prison, handcuffed and in charge of an officer. I can only hope that my failure with him will result in some attempt at psychological treatment and not in punishment.

14th August

A depressing day. Visited X prison. Found Bill scrubbing floors. I imagined he had gone to the other prison for sympathetic treatment. Instead he is at the mercy of warders at X prison . . . Poor Bill just sat and cried when he saw me.

An afternoon at X prison. Bill is still there doing manual work. If he is treated as he is being treated much longer he will become more violent and suicidal and later he will develop into a 'monster who attacks defenceless women and young girls', for whose punishment by the cat our society women call out.[1]

[1] Bill received a sentence of a flogging and imprisonment for attempted rape with violence shortly after his release.

II

THE MULTIPLICITY OF
DELINQUENCY

Dr. John Bowlby, Psychiatrist in charge of the Child Guidance Unit at the Tavistock Clinic, introduces his valuable report on "Forty-four Juvenile Thieves"[1] thus :

'Planned team research is of the utmost value, as has been demonstrated during the war, but no good plan can be made without adequate preliminary reconnaissance. Without such reconnaissance large-scale research can only be a waste of time and a waste of money. Normally scientific research into a problem goes through at least three major phases—the correct formulation of the problem and the bright idea, the further exploration of the problem and the framing of a hypothesis, and finally, the planned research designed to test the hypothesis. Whilst psycho-analysts have sometimes been guilty of supposing that phases one and two were sufficient, social psychologists and sociologists have often tended to skip these phases, and go straight into a piece of statistically planned research without adequate examination of the problem and without having framed a reasonable hypothesis. *As a result each party has hitherto had little use for the other's work.* It is much to be hoped that a clearer recognition of the value of the different phases of research will lead to close and active collaboration in the future.'

There are dozens of books on juvenile delinquency; dozens of sets of conclusions; classifications of causes and predisposing

[1] John Bowlby, M.A., M.D. (Cantab.), *Forty-four Juvenile Thieves, Their Characters and Home Life.* Ballière, Tindall and Cox. 1946.

20

influences; anecdotal stories and sympathetic accounts of behaviour observed in Juvenile Courts and problem homes; dozens of theories of delinquency based on more or less specialised experience in dealing with it *as a problem*; in sociological and psychological literature, hundreds of detailed and objective factual accounts of delinquents, their environments and their personal history. Documentary films have recently been shown on the subject. A recent play *Now Barabbas* takes young offenders inside prison as its central characters; the playwright has been in prison (for refusal to attack a civilian occupied French town), and he says:[1]

'I studied some two or three thousand prisoners during my stay in two English gaols, and I arrived at the conclusion that no more than 10 per cent were "criminals", by which I mean, to use the Bible's phraseology, "men possessed of devils" that could never be cast out ... I contend that, for the remaining 90 per cent a medical and not a punitive approach is far more likely to effect a cure.'

What a sample for a statistician, and what an opportunity for a Mass-Observer! The author, Mr. W. Douglas Home, is a keen observer himself, but the requirements of drama restrict the aspects of 'delinquent' life he can present. He cannot show the typical: an hour or two spent speechlessly kicking a tin from gutter to gutter outside his parents' home, unable to go in because a quarrel is on, or just because there isn't room; such monotonous and undramatic actions may fill the background years out of which the first tense delinquent moments finally spring. Prison, or Borstal, like life itself, becomes really dramatic on fairly rare occasions, and then often because someone's nerve has snapped through the long intervening period of montony.

Outside Borstal? A national survey by Dr. Mark Abrams [2] on the use people make of their leisure time shows that 23 per cent of boys aged 16 to 20, delinquent and otherwise, say they spend their spare time doing 'Nothing'. These negative unmemorable activities break down, under observation, into several quite

---

[1] *Picture Post*, 15th March 1947.
[2] Quoted in *News Review*, 12th December 1947.

distinct groups. Sociologically speaking 'Doing nothing' is not a very useful classification for the activities of nearly a quarter of the nation's youth. But that is how they put it themselves, and it tells us a good deal about their *attitude* to the use they make of their spare time.

Delinquency and Youth, then, are one of the main focuses of attention to-day. They are being studied statistically, psychologically, journalistically, by magistrates, magistrates' clerks, welfare workers, club leaders, clergy; written about by anyone and everyone in every sort of medium from learned journal to woman's magazine, textbook to Penguin book.

Here is some more writing about Youth and Delinquency. The chief object of this Mass-Observation report is to introduce members of that substantial section of the community who are, or aren't quite, juvenile delinquents, to those who have not met any; or, if they have, have met them under circumstances where their behaviour and conversation is rather different from its unselfconcious norm.

In making the survey we have been struck by one fact especially. The more closely concerned with delinquency people have been, the less inclined have they been to generalise, or even to categorise. As the Director of Borstal, Mr. R. Y. Bradley, put it :

'I've been in this work for 23 years and I don't know the causes yet. However many individuals may come into a Borstal, there are that number of individual causes.'

Those concerned with the development of new methods of treating delinquents particularly stressed to us the fact that a diversity of views between experts at this stage was to be expected, and that more harm than good would be done by emphasising these differences.

A wide area of agreement exists over the multiplicity of the *causes* of delinquency. The implication—that a greater differentiation between the types of treatment at the state's disposal is needed—has, of course, been the basis of criminal reform for a generation. Early reforms were broadly humanitarian. The idea of retribution and revenge had to weaken before the idea of cure could begin to take its place. It is only in quite recent years that the conception of constructive treatment has begun to penetrate the laws and regulations determining what happens to a person after conviction.

Rapid and fundamental changes have taken place in the past few decades in the whole conception of individual responsibility, whose full implications are only just beginning to be realised. It is hardly surprising if, in a field which touches the most intimate susceptibilities of most of us, practice has not kept pace with theory. On the basic assumption that all is not well in our treatment of crime, there is little knowledgeable disagreement. Disagreement comes in deciding which aspects of present practice should be scrapped, or augmented; and most especially in deciding with what new facilities they should be replaced or extended.

The delinquency *problem* (like the whole crime problem), then, is still in an exploratory stage. As Sir Cyril Burt[1] puts it :

'Crime is the outcome of many confluents. How wide a variety of adverse causes may contribute to youthful delinquency is graphically shown by the figures I have given. In all, more than 170 distinct conditions have been encountered, every one often conclusive to childish misconduct.'

'On an average, each delinquent child is the product of nine or ten subversive circumstances, one as a rule predominating, and all conspiring to draw him into crime.'

Cure, as opposed to the suppression of symptoms, cannot be assured until provision is made for dealing with all these numerous factors which predispose the child to delinquency. The causes themselves are as yet only inadequately understood, and an understanding of cause is only the first step towards devising a cure. While it is only too simple to point at aspects of existing systems for dealing with criminals, young or old, which appear 'obviously wrong', to do so may be worse than useless if there is no alternative which is equally 'obviously right'.

Some may feel that the present contribution suffers from this defect. In our material—only a small part of which is used here—there is case after case in which young people undergoing institutional treatment or serving prison sentences appear to be

[1] *The Young Delinquent*, Cyril Burt, University of London Tutorial Press, 1931.

left almost entirely untouched, not only in regard to cure, but in regard to any salutary alleviation of symptoms in the interests of society. Where the delinquent is quite clearly motivated by something entirely beyond his control or comprehension, one is tempted to pass judgement on a system that subjects him for several years to disciplinary treatment and moralistic exhortation that stands no apparent chance of overcoming his uncontrollable urge, yet provides no means of systematically and sympathetically attempting to unravel his mind. Such a case is that of Bill, already quoted.

But it must be constantly borne in mind that for a very considerable number of 'recidivists' no 'right' treatment yet exists, in the sense of one which will effect a certain, or even a probable, cure. If a case appears ostentatiously 'psychological', that does not mean that psychological treatments are necessarily available to cure it; any more than discipline and order are sure-fire cures for delinquencies arising from indiscipline and disorder. Diagnosis may be simple, but the prognosis in our present state of knowledge, may be 'hopeless'.

The whole idea of a young offender against society who, *for no fault of his own,* is virtually predestined to a life of crime, is a conception very difficult to assimilate, since it cuts across all sorts of long-held basic social values. In the case of Bill, for instance, the problem is not solved by the merely humanitarian measure of providing more sympathetic treatment for him during his period of confinement. There still remains the question of what should happen then. If he is virtually certain to repeat the offence for which he came in very soon after his release, should he be released, since society and he himself will suffer? On the other hand, what possible just-seeming reason can be devised for keeping him in confinement after he has served his legal sentence? Should the lunacy laws be revised to include people like Bill? Or should our whole conception of justice be revised to provide an indeterminate period of treatment for all offenders against given laws, until such time as they are deemed fit for society and safe to themselves? Either suggestion carries alarming potentialities.

These are the sort of problems which will have to be faced

if and when prisons and institutions really become places of cure instead of the present uneasy mixture of treatment, deterrent, and punishment. That time is remote. The immediate problem is still one of delineating—of finding out who, what and why? This report merely aims at presenting some material of a rather different sort from that which has usually been presented elsewhere.

We shall not attempt here to draw conclusions, to make generalisations, or to suggest remedies, reforms or treatments. There is a big blank in the literature of delinquency between occasional *realistic* type-character studies and the work of more or less specialised observers who see delinquents only under special circumstances and in special environments. Bill Naughton's portrait of a Spiv is a classic example of the former. Since his original article appeared in *Pilot Papers,* and was reproduced in the *News Chronicle,* a new word has been added to the language. But it is a word of numerous, often incompatible, connotations as it is used in popular journalism. Naughton's 'Spiv' was a generic type, not an individual. To those less intimately acquainted with this subject than Bill Naughton a considerable section of young men of the working class seems nowadays to belong to the 'Spiv' type.

The current blank is the flesh-and-blood presentation of the ordinary delinquent himself. His absence is due to two main factors:

1. That much of the literature of the subject is written by specialists for specialists.

2. That much of the rest is written for more popular consumption, by people who do not really know their subject *at that level.*

Dr. Bowlby has provided the model disclaimer for 'unsystematic' work in his preface to a far more systematic study than the present one. He says: 'The number of cases is small; the constitution of the sample chancy, the recording of dates unsystematic, the amount of data on different cases uneven. Conclusions drawn in such circumstances are clearly liable to all sorts of errors.' We echo these sentiments in respect of this brief survey, which aims to describe a little, not to generalise about a lot.

However, what Dr. Bowlby says about the relation between

psychiatrist and social psychologist, the complementary *potential* of their work, and the actual existing *attitude*—'Each party has hitherto had little use for the other's work'—applies equally to the relationship between mass-observer and opinion poller, between M-O's type of research and the type generally known as 'Public Opinion Research'. Indeed, the finality with which some psychologists sometimes pronounce conclusions in fields where little detailed exploratory work has been done is astonishing. It was an eminent psychologist, not an opinion poll, who allowed to be released as statistical fact the astounding information that Socialists don't expect another war and Conservatives do. Statistical method, applied *before* preliminary reconnaissance has provided a well-documented hypothesis to test, may lead to 'conclusions' as tendentious as any that arise from qualitative studies of fairly typical cases. The statistics may be accurate; but statistics are often meaningless until they are interpreted, and interpretation depends on knowledge from *outside* the statistics—of qualities as well as quantities. Where that knowledge is tenuous or lacking, figures can easily lie. [1]

Thus statistics 'proved' that the disease beri-beri was germ-borne, for it had epidemic qualities and spread in limited territorial areas. For years scientists examined water supplies and other possible sources of infection in an attempt to trace the organism, till finally it was discovered that beri-beri is a deficiency disease. Its rapid spread in certain areas was due to the localisation of nutritional deficiencies, dependent on food crops. The statistics were correct, but they were meaningless without interpretation. The 'obvious' interpretation was wrong; the result long delayed an elucidation of the problem the figures were collected to solve.

Discussing Carr-Saunders, Mannheim and Rhodes *Young Offenders*—the fullest statistical survey of delinquency in this country—Dr. Bowlby suggests that because all types of delinquent are there considered together, trends which might have been highly significant if different groups had been treated

---

[1] For discussion of this subject see Introduction by N. D. Willcock to Mass-Observation *Peace and the Public Mind* (Longmans 1947), and Tom Harrison's 'The Nature of Sociology' in *Pilot Papers*, March 1947.

separately 'may well have become obscured or even obliterated'. These authors' own qualification of the value of a statistical approach to problems of delinquency reads:

'Whilst making a strong plea for continuous research of a statistical nature under these three heads, *we desire to utter a warning against expecting that statistics can solve the whole of the problems.*[1]

When it is a question, for example, of the fluctuation in the frequency of delinquency as a whole, and must be sought from those practised in the watching of general changes in social habit and attitude, statistical methods are invaluable aids in the solution of social problems, but statisticians are well aware that their methods are not enough.' (*Young Offenders,* p. 159.)

The phrase 'frequency of delinquency as a whole' rather by-passes the issue. Those 'practised in the watching of general changes in social habit and attitude' are only too well aware that 'delinquency as a whole' is a statistical abstraction which befogs the reality, like smoking-as-a-whole, matrimony-as-a-whole, or eating-as-a-whole. In the case of delinquency the 'whole' is an arbitrary bundle of symptoms whose only common factor lies in the fact that it is 'agin the law' to allow them expression. It is a delinquent act to steal an apple because you are hungry, to smash windows because you are bored, to murder the headmaster because you dislike him, or to rape a girl because you 'can't help it'. Vacillations in the incidence of delinquency-as-a-whole remain meaningless abstractions—as meaningless as vacillations in the birthrate, the divorce rate or the Labour vote—until the symptoms bundled under the all-embracing generic word are disentangled, described and classified. Only then is it possible to see *what* is vacillating; and only after the 'what?' is adequately answered do we know where to look for the 'why?'

Four out of every six juvenile delinquents brought before the courts for indictable offences are thieves. The vast majority are boys. The peak age for delinquency is thirteen. These are the top-level statistical facts. But if, from these statistics, it is

[1] Our italics.

27

deduced that the problem to be solved is one of theft, particularly during the year before leaving school, the focus can very easily be thrown out. Measures may then be taken, as indeed they are clearly being taken, to stop theft. The holes through which we address cashiers and booking clerks may become, as they are becoming, daily smaller and less accessible, the protective bars and unsmashable glass thicker, till finally invisible cashiers may be addressed through a microphone and our change come through a one-way steel tube from some distant strong-room. And theft may continue (as it is continuing now) to increase, because the many internal pressures of which theft can be a symptom remain as acute as ever.

If we take a look at a few juvenile thieves, not necessarily 'tpical' or a 'random sample', it immediately becomes apparent that we are looking at a group of quite different people. They have in common the fact that they have stolen something, but in describing *what* they are, this common factor may well seem of small significance in comparison with the disparities and differences we find.

Dr. Bowlby is among the first to have taken such a group and to have described in detail not only their overt differences and similarities, of behaviour, environment, etc., but the hidden differences and similarities which only prolonged therapeutic treatment can systematically uncover. Dr. Edward Glover and his colleagues have done pioneer work in other parts of this field.

Why, then, should Mass-Observation worry? If modern psychiatry, with its highly developed techniques for unfolding individual motivations and untangling uncomprehended drives, is working on the problem, where does the sociological method of M-O come in?

There are three reasons:

1. The psycho-analyst is as much a special kind of specialist as, for instance, the magistrate or the social workers. Dr. Bowlby speaks of the 'factors of very great importance which only come to light after weeks of sympathetic discussion with a skilled worker'. These are factors which, it is true, might never come to light in discussion with a magistrate or a prison officer.

But they also include factors which have often *already* come to light in, say, the boy's letters to his girl friend, in conversation with his particular pals, or in his overt behaviour in his normal environment. In order to dig very deep systematically it is often necessary to remain at a shallow level for a long time. M-O, by assembling a collection of less systematic observational data and subjective case-histories, partly eliminates this all-important time factor, and may produce lines for enquiry, or hint at common factors, which a fully systematic depth-study of individuals has missed.

2. It is an important of M-O's job to present in recognisable form, to the widest possible public, those social habits, attitudes, institutions and individuals with whom it is dealing. This function is particularly important when the study is one of a section of the community little known to the majority. M-O aims not only at acquiring knowledge about ourselves, but at *spreading* this knowledge as widely as possible. The social sciences operate almost exclusively at an academic level. Knowledge of their findings penetrates downwards from academic circles largely through popularisers from outside the specialist field who may (or may not) present the facts correctly. Juvenile Delinquency, like any other social problem or phenomenon, is something which intimately concerns all our daily lives. M-O believes that it is part of its job to acquaint ordinary people with these facts, which are facts of use in everyday human relations, and have an incidental therapeutic value of their own.

3. Whatever facts are being found out at specialist levels, however incontrovertibly a truth may be established, the combined power of print, radio, screen and stage often distort the facts and implant some quite different set of ideas in people's minds. The established 'truth' never has been, and never will be, automatically accepted and incorporated. This is an additional reason why the social scientist should at all costs avoid academic seclusion, and it is especially applicable to-day.

The remainder of this report is, therefore, simply a CONTRIBUTION, the sketch of another approach to the subject. Even the small-scale collection of material in this way is arduous, and the present effort has been made possible only through the co-operation of many people with interests in this field. In particular, we were amazed by the degree of crypto-co-operation forthcoming from officials in the reformatory institutions, the more intelligent of whom are widely dissatisfied with the prevailing state of affairs. We have used our own wide field of contacts and our staff of whole-time investigators to throw the net as wide as possible. But this remains primarily a collection of individual cases for consideration. We hope to pursue the problem further in the near future. Meanwhile, those interested in this type of research can see what other sorts of research we have done and are doing in the appendix at the end of this report.

III

EVERYONE A DELINQUENT

'A child is to be regarded as technically delinquent when his anti-social tendencies appear so grave that he becomes or ought to become, the object of official action.' (Cyril Burt.)

A respectable middle-aged citizen, an electrician, admitted —(informally and anonymously—*not* as a result of a questionnaire) :

1. That he took bars of soap from his workplace, 'whenever, and as often as, I can'.

2. That he had taken books of foolscap paper from work, as well as electric wire.

3. That he sometimes fiddled money from electric meters which he had to open in the course of his job.

4. That he had taken beer glasses from various pubs.

5. That he had sold 15 stolen watches.

6. That he had often travelled on the railway for a long journey without a ticket and only paid for a short journey.

Becoming interested in the variety of his delinquences, he recalled the following incidents :

7. 'I went to Woolworths about a year ago—picked up four packets of seeds, hid one in my hand, and only paid for three. I did it intentionally.'

8. 'I was in hospital two years ago. I gave visitors things to bring, and when I left, I brought home a few things myself— towels, handkerchiefs, a pillow case, a sheet and a pair of shoes for myself.'

A woman, equally respectable :

'I often used to take sweets from shops when I was a young

girl. Lately I've taken toilet paper from women's lavatories I've been to—there was a shortage of it a little while ago. When I was working in a pub part time, I used occasionally to take packets of cigarettes—I gave them to my husband. Everyone else used to take them so I thought I might as well.'

Two lists of stolen property in the homes of young middle-class citizens.

LIST A

1. One book acquired from a R.A.F. Station.
2. One flying jacket ('A magnificent achievement, having been withdrawn from stores prior to de-mob.')
3. One box of '—Hotel' notepaper.
4. One pair of Rugby boots which I found.
5. One R.A.F. Rugby jersey.
6. Few pencils and blotting paper from Ministry of—

LIST B

1. 'Vat 69' bottle from local pub.
2. 2 pairs forks and spoons, stolen by a friend from the army.
3. Music, from music teacher.
4. Paint and paper from a school at which I taught.
5. Ball of string from a pub.
6. Postcards and magazine from present workplace.
7. Portfolio—from University department.
8. A revolver and a seal—from relatives.
9. The last and bulkiest item comes a little outside the range of ordinary respectable delinquency and we leave it blank!

As a young man of seventeen put it :
'I've taken expensive chemical apparatus from work—that's not really stealing, though, is it?'

For other tastes, other exceptions. The boy whose early and less ambitious delinquencies are described by himself later in this report, started by making an exception of toffee, biscuits, and chocolate. Books are a safer proposition. Lending libraries do not place gold watches on their shelves or leave the petty cash about, and since they may be legally entered for illegal purposes at any time, a book-thief has the advantage of comparative secrecy and a lack of direct temptation to extend his range of larceny. Institutions and workplaces share the library's advantage of open access, while lavatories, main hunting-ground of the non-delinquent thief, provide complete secrecy of operation, though the range of choice is limited.

The Evening News (22nd January 1947) reports : 'Police are investigating a series of systematic thefts from three West London public libraries, involving the loss of more than 700 books. One person is believed to be responsible, as in each case at Ealing, Acton, Brentford and Chiswick libraries only the best fiction has been stolen. An early arrest is expected, as Ealing's librarian points out "it is not easy to camouflage the books".'

Ealing's librarian may be right about the difficulty of camouflaging books, yet 700 seems a fair haul for one individual who, if he stops now, may well remain 'non-delinquent'. One London Public Library, checking its stock for the first time since the war, found over 1,000 books missing in the fiction section alone. During the war, working on salvage collection, the librarian here returned many thousands of books to over twenty main public libraries from Southampton to Edinburgh. When Loughborough Public Library held a 'moratorium week', with no questions asked and no fines imposed, the result was the return of one book for every thirty residents. Bookthieves' consciences quiet frequently cause them to return to the scene of the crime —in the above-mentioned library some book which has been missing for between five and twenty years reappears on the shelves about once in every ten days.

We chanced on an exceptional month to collect these petty-theft statistics from a popular restaurant. The month's losses were :

1 sugar sifter	19 spoons
7 forks	10 ash trays

Said our informant: 'This is quite an exception, though. We usually have about 30 or 40 knives and 10 dessert spoons missing as well. Ash trays seem to have a big attraction for some of the people.'

A bookshop assistant in charge of an open display reports a loss of 5 or 6 books a week from theft. 'They nearly always take the books about sex.' And from a famous London shop, largely patronised by middle and upper class people.

'The cheap stuff—thin paper novels, mostly pornography—I should say about twelve a week go. Not many new books are stolen. Saturday's the worst day. Anything from 2 to 6 or 7 might go. It depends on the assistant you know. The people would soon take them if the assistant wasn't looking.

There's no particular type that takes them. All types do really, you know. You'd be surprised sometimes at the people that do take them—quite well-to-do they are often. People who needn't steal—quiet usually they are.'

During the war we have all become familiar with the effect of scarcity on petty theft. But, though the rise is starting, the norm was not low. An average of about one railway towel a year to every seventh household in the country was delinquently acquired during the year 1939—40. Such statistics could be multiplied, emphasising the delinquent latent in all of us. Far and away the most frequent charges before the Juvenile Courts are ones of petty theft. The difference between 'them' and 'us' is often no more than that the 'delinquent' has stolen under conditions of personal risk, while more respectable citizens confine themselves usually to thefts from libraries, lavatories, institutions, workplaces and hotels, which are exceedingly unlikely to be detected, or if detected, prosecuted.

The dividing line between 'respectable' and 'reprehensible' delinquency is an almost impossible one to draw. Thus a middle-class housewife, one of many who nowadays tips their tradesmen:

'I only give it because I feel like doing so. I don't expect anything in return, although I wouldn't say no if it was offered. Lots of people do give tips to shopkeepers to get extra rations—you won't get them to admit it though.'

Many, perhaps most, people do something sometimes which is against the law, even if it is only souvenir hunting, the theft of some lavatory paper, purloining some stationery from a hotel, or accepting an extra pint from the milkman.

Respectable delinquency is *almost* safe from prosecution just because it has become respectable on account of its accepted frequency. Or else it is undertaken at rather more risk, under pressure of circumstance. The middle classes, living far below their accustomed standard of plenty, venture in on the fringe of the black market, not quite so safely.

But when the standard of poorer people falls through force of circumstances, then the way out is less simple, more dangerously illegal. Many young people who serve a sentence in an institution have probably no more, if not fewer, 'delinquent traits' to their character than thousands of others whom circumstance does not tempt so strongly. They emerge from their sentence 'cured', and account for an unknown proportion of the success figures of institutional and prison treatment.

Here are descriptions of two such cases, as recorded in a padre's diary:

1

11th October

Interviewed young D., the married man. He enquired about confirmation. His wife, he said, had been confirmed and he would like to be, for her sake. But he was a little doubtful about his ability to stay the course, if he were confirmed, for, he said, 'You are not allowed to smoke if you are confirmed, are you?'

He had married 'to make his wife an honest woman' to avoid a bastard child. He had then produced another. The father of two and unable to obtain work as a dock labourer in Birkenhead at a man's wage, as he is under 21, he had gone a-stealing out of sheer concern for his wife and kids. With the result of 'Three years Borstal.' Meanwhile his wife exists on 27s. 6d. a week Public Assistance grant, and pays 10 shillings a week rent, and feeds and clothes herself and the children and writes cheerful encouraging letters to her husband twice a week.

Saw Mrs. D. who had come on a 'Morris visit' to see her husband. The Public Assistance Board has decreased her allowance from 27s. 6d. a week to 25 shillings because she did not report the absence of her baby boy in hospital for a few days. So she now subsists on 25 shillings a week and asks pathetically when she may expect her man home. He is ready to go now, he had his jolt and means to steal no more. That—in his case it is a fact—will be so at the end of another year. He will not intend to steal any more earnestly than he does to-day.

2

14th February

Talked with H. He is to all intents and purposes an orphan, who has had to keep himself. He is an artist and a musician, a gentle lover of beauty. He passed a stiffish exam. at the age of 17 to qualify for a Civil Service job in the Post Office. At the age of 21, for six weeks out of seven, his work was night work as a sorter, typical shifts being 6 a.m. to 2 p.m., 5.15 p.m. to 12.45 a.m., 7.30 p.m. to 2.45 a.m. . . . . and every few weeks Sunday 7.30 p.m. to 6 a.m. Monday. His wages were 37 shillings. His board and lodging 25 shillings. He stole money orders, of a few shillings worth. Otherwise he has a blameless record. 'You held a position of trust', said the judge, 'so you must have three years of Borstal training.'

A position of trust at 37 shillings a week! His appearance in court would have been sufficient cure for him. Three months in Borstal would have done equally much for him as his two years he has been kept here.

IV

KICKING A TIN AROUND

Twenty three per cent of the nation's youth, when asked what they do in their spare time, say 'Nothing', according to Dr. Abrams' survey, previously mentioned. When he asked young people in a London borough a more specific question about how they had spent the previous evening, their main activities broke down as follows:[1]

	per cent
In the cinema	21
Club, etc.	8
Helping in house	8
Indoors	8
Reading	7
Dancing	7
Working	7
Walking in street	5
Show or concert	5

This leaves us with 24 per cent miscellaneous and negative activities, much the same group as Dr. Abrams' 23 per cent 'Doing Nothing'. But 'walking the street', the evening occupation of 5 per cent of all young people in this borough and one in every fourteen of the boys, is somewhat arbitrarily extracted from the negative group. Some 15,000 youths aged 14-20 walking the streets of London as their main occupation on a typical weekday evening—a fraction of the more specific ways of doing nothing memorable—this is one aspect of one part of the background to delinquency. Let us glance at this behavioural segment first.

[1] Miscellaneous activities, 'doing nothing', etc., have been omitted, therefore the percentage does not add up to 100.

What do they do, these young people with nothing to do but walk around?

The answers are very various, and can only be indicated by a few typical observations.

Street.

Here, for instance, is an hour or so from the life of a 13-year-old boy, observed in a London suburb:

A boy scruffily dressed in P. Street. He has very long hair hanging all over his face, hands in pockets and both eyes on the ground. He is walking slowly to and fro across the road, and with every other step he takes he kicks before him a large cardboard box. Keeping to the same narrow stretch of road he keeps up this crossing and kicking for 15 minutes. Then he turns in the middle of the road and walks and kicks down for about 15 yards. Then he starts again to and fro across the road, hands in pockets, head down, gazing at the ground, kicking the box before him still at every other step. As soon as he gets to the curb, he turns about and continues until reaching the other curb and so goes on. He keeps this up for another 20 minutes or so, during which time two cars come along. He takes no notice of them, in fact he seems to walk even slower as they approach, and the cars consequently have to slow down and wait for him to get out of the way. He seems oblivious of their presence because he does not look at them at all—luckily the street is well lighted so he can easily be seen.

Suddenly kicking the box into the curb he walks towards C. Street and continues to slouch along, still hands in pockets and head down looking at the ground. He stops in front of a restaurant and looks inside through the window. He stays there for four minutes, just staring inside. Apparently he is looking at the brightly lit and gaily decorated Christmas tree which is at the far end of the shop. He walks on again slowly, reaching a tube station. He turns right and goes down into an underground public lavatory. Comes out after 15 minutes and walks back to P. Street. Goes into a side street and into a house.

38

And here is a typical series of short observations of street groups :

1

Just around the corner from the Angel Station are two youths, males, ages 15 and 16. They are leaning on the railings separating the pavement from the road, and conversing in whispers. Suddenly one shouts out 'Garn—Bet I can' and climbs on to the top rail and proceeds to balance himself and 'tight rope walk' along it. He loses his balance after a few yards and jumps into the road, a car nearly hitting him. He turns to his friend saying, 'All right—now let's see you do it.' His friend also climbs up and walks along the rail. They do this in turn, seeing who can walk the further without falling off. They were still here half an hour later, balancing as before, when investigator passed this way.

2

Outside a pub in some back streets west of Upper Street are 7 youths—5 males 15-18 years of age and 2 females 16-17 years of age. They are in a group, some of them leaning against the wall of the pub. The two girls are heavily made up, one of them appears to investigator to have dyed blonde hair. The other is a natural blonde. They are both wearing dresses and coats, with their hands in the pockets. The boys are all wearing overcoats, collars turned up and usually with hands in pockets.

Four of the boys are talking in a group whilst the other one is playing about with one of the girls. He is holding her by the arms pressing her back against the wall, and at the same time kissing her. She laughs and screams whilst the other girl looks on and passes comments. These two continue to push one another about for several minutes, he occasionally pushing her against the wall and then kissing her. The other girl still stands near by, just looking at them and passing remarks.

The four boys are still conversing in a group, then two of them break away and start to wrestle with each other, to the verbal encouragement of the other two. After a minute or two they stopped and gathered in a circle under a street lamp and start to laugh and talk, the two girls especially laughing almost continually and very harshly and loudly.

3

All around C-Station there are groups of young people either walking about in groups or else standing in doorways or on street corners. It seems more noticeable here than in any other part of London.

One group of 3 girls and 2 boys, ages about 14-16 are sitting on the chains which separate the pavement from the road, and are swinging to and fro. The five of them are all talking and giggling in very harsh voices. Every now and again the girls shout at the boys, 'Garn, who do you think I am?' 'Oh, shut up.' 'Bugger off.' The boys laugh loudly at this and start to catch hold of the girls, while the girls try to shake them off and renew their protestations. This sort of thing goes on for about 15 minutes.

One of the girls, still swinging on the chains, yodels loudly and waves her hand at someone in — — road. All except one are smoking. The girls are all extremely heavily made up, with extra thick lipstick applied carelessly. Two of them are wearing slacks, the other a short length dress. The boys are both wearing overcoats. They can't be more than 14. Their hair is rather uncontrollable but they have applied lots of water, with the result that it is all 'cakey'. Two of the girls leave, the remaining one still sits on the chains with a boy on either side of her. They are talking and giggling.

Five girls walk by on the other side of the road and whistle to the two boys, who take no notice. They are all 14-15—heavily made-up, two with dyed blonde hair. They are marching along arm-in-arm, spread out across the pavement, singing 'Give Me Five Minutes More'. They look in the doorway at me and whistle and pass comments amongst themselves, giggle, and walk off still singing and humming. The other three are still hanging round the chains. They are still there 1½ hrs. later, when I pass.

There are many other males and females in groups and

40

single, some standing in doorways and talking, some just looking at the people passing by. There are groups of semi-spiv types and the like just strolling around, hands in pockets, going nowhere in particular, just walking along the street and going into cafés and amusement arcades, or else standing for hours on end at street corners or in shop doorways.'

'Having Nothing Else to Do'

The beginning of a delinquent career may arise out of such aimless street activity. Take two bottle-smashing episodes. The first is an observation, one of many similar observations, from a working-class suburb. The second is an early reminiscence of a Borstal lad, telling how his history of delinquency began:

1

Two youths, ages about 18, are standing outside a dairy. They pick up between them a large crate of empty milk bottles and throw them into the road, breaking all of them (about 20). They start to laugh, and then run across the road and join a gang of youths numbering about 15 or 16. Most of them are dressed very flashily—striped flannels and 'house coat' style of belted jacket; large, loosely knotted, plain coloured ties; and several of them are wearing the wide-brimmed American style of trilby. Long 'side-boards' are a prominent feature with the majority of them. A policeman comes on the scene and asks questions, but nobody seems to know anything. He continues to walk up and down for a while.

2

'I was sixteen years of age when I first struck a bad patch. It began like this. It was 10.30 on a wet cold day, the snow was falling thick and fast and I could not see a yard ahead and my companions were in the same condition when we came to a coal yard which we all knew and we went in to ask the man in charge if we could shelter in one of the old sheds until the snow had abated a bit and he being a good samaritan said we could. We thank him and off we went into the old shed. The

41

first thing I did when I got inside was take off my raincoat and deposit it upon a nail which was at the back of the door, having done that I sat down upon a desk which was on the far side of the shed and started a conversation with one of my friends. Everything went well for the first half-hour, then one of the boys found a lot of bottles in a corner and *having nothing else to do* put them up in a line and began to shy at them until he broke them all. He was not appeased in having broken all the bottles, he picked up a rusty piece of iron and began to break the windows in the place. I told him to pack it up as the owner would naturally take offense at what he had done; he told me to go to hell in not a decent way and I took the tip and left in a hurry, in such a hurry however that I had left behind my raincoat and I turned back to get it. When I got there one of the workmen were then taking the names of all the fellows there. I asked what was wrong and he pounced on me also getting my name. He took me round the shed and I was awestruck at what they had done: there was not a single thing in the shed that had not been smashed. He then sais to me you will hear more of this and now get out the lot of you.

'I went off on my own and dismissed the whole thing from my mind. The same night as I was going to the pictures there came a knock on our door and I being nearest answered the knock, imagine my surprise at seeing a policeman at the door with the owner of the coal yard. May we come in please and I said yes in a funny voice. He said I have comes to see you about the shed you had a hand in wrecking it, your pals has told us all about it. I was very indignant at being accused of something, I had not done and I sais so so he said it is no good you will have to tell a better story than that. You will appear in court on Wednesday, which is two days away.

'Wednesday came and I went to the court confident that I could prove that I had nothing to do with the job of wrecking the shed as they put it. I was waiting to hear my case called and at last it came I got up and went through the routine and then it began I told the court what had really happened and they said it is five against yourself. My pals were determined that I should be dragged in.

'I got twelve months probation on the charge of wilful damage and my name splashed in a newspaper column. I finished my probation and was getting on all right again for the first three months and then there came a drop in the trade and I was one of many to get on the dole. It was while I was up there signing on that I met a school friend who also had struck a bad patch we got chatting and he said what about going farther away from here to get a job we got bikes ain't we and we can use 'em so come with me tomorrow and we will go to brum. I said not so fast my cycles smashed up so that lets me out, in that case you can borrow our kids he wont mind so be ready in the morning by half past six.

'The next morning came and sure enough he came with two cycles and off we went. We both got a job at the same place and we were both in highspirits going back home. I said come to our house and have a cup of tea which he did so. We had just sat down when there came a loud knock at the door and my mother answered it, when she came back she said to me a detective wants to see you Wilf, a little surprised I went out to him and he greeted me with this—a nice bicycle you have. I said to him it does not belong to me and he said no who does it belong to. I told him it belonged to my friends brother he said is your friend with you and I said yes, can I see him says he and I called him to come outside a minute.

'When he came he was a bit pale and I said do you feel ill. I suppose he does says the tec. he knows me very well and out comes the whole lot about the bicycles and I was again summoned for being in possession of a stolen cycle I went to court and got another year on pro. they would not listen to me, and I went out into the street a very bitter man. I there and then made up my mind to do something and get done for it than do nothing and get done. So off I went and stole a ladies furcoat. I did not want it so I gave it to a rag and bone man, he in his turn took it to the police and the police came for me and I admitted the case. I went to the sessions and get three years Borstal. I did nearly two years and was let out, but while I was in there I made some good friends and I also thought of the injustice done to me.'

Cinema

According to Dr. Abrams' survey more than a third of young men aged 16-20 attend the cinema once a week. Almost a quarter of them go twice weekly, while nearly 20 per cent go three times.

In our London survey we found that the cinema was far and away the favourite youth leisure activity. Asked what they *usually* did in the evening, over half of the young people mentioned cinema-going, and 41 per cent said it was one of their usual ways of spending the week-end. When we asked them what sort of things they spent their money on, these were the main items which came into their minds:[1]

	per cent
Cinemas, shows, amusements	59
Clothes	23 (chiefly girls)
Savings	22 (chiefly boys)
Cigarettes, sweets, snacks	21
Make-up, etc.	9 (all girls—18 per cent of them)
Sport, rambling	9
Essentials and Home	9
Books and reading matter	7

One of the few sound sociological studies which has been made of the effect of films on young people (HERBERT BLUMER and PHILIP M. HAUSER, *Movies, Delinquency and Crime,* New York, Macmillan, 1933) concludes :

'The child in the high rate delinquency area tends to be sensitised and the child in the low-rate delinquency area immunised to delinquent and criminal attitudes and forms of behaviour depicted on the screen. On the other hand, the forms of thought and behaviour presented by the movies are such as to provide material and incentive to those sensitised to delinquent and criminal suggestions.'

It is hardly to be expected that delinquents will themselves spontaneously blame the cinema for their actions. More indirect stresses are likely to be relevant.

[1] Many young people mentioned more than one item, so that percentages add to over 100.

44

Here is a young habitual delinquent's early memory of a cowboy film. He saw the film *at least five years before he wrote this account of it,* and it is clear that this impression, whatever its repercussions, was very deep.

'Ma cuts me a couple of sanwiges and pours me a cup of tea and I rushes through the light snack and off to the pictures I go, and call for a couple of pals of mine until there is a little crowd of us, and we discuss the ending of last weeks part of a seriel, and we disides to let him know when the gangster's are behind him. So we lines up to go in, and when we go in we shout we want buck or we want our money back, so he makes a start with the seriel, we see as he falls off the bridge he makes a grab at the bridge and judges correctly and he pulls himself back up and runs after the gangsters.

'So one of the gangsters look round and see buck coming after them, so they start fireing at him, so buck darts behind the tresslis and takes a shot at one of the gangsters and shoots him in the leg, then the gangsters see the pose coming and tries to make a break for it but soon the pose catches all of them but the chief and buck seeing his horse coming with the pose gives chase after the chief and the chief reaches his horse and rides away to the mountains, so buck follows in pursuit, and buck urges his horse to his fastest pace and buck gradually gains on the chief until they are high up in the mountains, and the chief finds he cannot go any further, so he jumps off his horse and takes a couple of shots at buck until he emptys his gun, so he trows it away and makes a grab for his rifle.

'But buck say drop it or Ill shoot so the chief drops riffle, and Buck closes, and ties him to his horse and they start going back to meet the pose and all of a soden the chief spurs his hors and the horse gallops away and reach the rivin to late so the cheif and the horse goes over the rivin just as buck reaches the edge and he sees the horse and chief hit the water, so buck rides back to the pose and tells them that the chief is dead, and so ends the serial and then we have a comic picture and we nearly laughs ourselves to death. So after the picture is over I pretends I am snowball and shoots the gangsters away and me pall wont play

45

with me any more because he wants to be buck, I says you cant be buck Jones cos your name is Richard you can be Gordon Richards a cousin to me so he agrees and we go riding home and I asks him to come in with me while I have something to eat.

'So I goes in and have my dinner and I cut a piece of cake for my pall and I says we will get our guns and have a game in the park, so we put our cowboy clothes on and races down the park, and jumps on the swings and we shoot at one another as we pass, then we slackens down and goes on the rounderbout and we makes it go round fast and we jumps on it and shoot at one another on it until the first one gets off. At half past five we go home for tea and after tea we go and have a game of kick the tin and run till supper time then my brother tells me its time to go in to get a bath, and after I have had my bath ma says dont go out again cos your supper will be ready soon, and I says to ma its only half past eight supper will be half an hour yet so ma gives in and say dont get dirty or you'll have another bath so I cuts in on a game of kick the tin and run till 9 o'clock and I have my supper and goes to bed.'

A youthful sense of adventure may be canalised into delinquent or near-delinquent forms by such impressions in a 'harmless' enough way at first, but with potential developments under the influence of discipline, 'misunderstanding', possible prosecution for escapades arising from childish fantasy and fun. Not enough is known about the effects of films on children for a generalisation to be possible. But a more indirect approach to the subject than has been made hitherto might be rewarding. What incidents in what films, seen how long ago, for instance, remain in the minds of young delinquents, and what apparent bearing have these memories on their own lives?

This lad became a housebreaker ...

Dance Hall

Among the more organised leisure pleasures of young people, dancing takes a fairly low second place to cinema-going. Dr. Abrams' national survey finds about a third of youth saying they spend their spare time in cinemas or dance halls. In our London survey we asked: 'What do you usually do at the week-end?' This generalised question produced about the same proportion —20 per cent—saying 'Nothing special' as did Dr. Abrams' general question on leisure. But two-fifths mentioned the cinema among their usual week-end activities, and one-fifth dancing. More specifically, asked what they had actually done on the previous evening, 21 per cent said they had been to the cinema, and 7 per cent to a dance.

The large dance-halls which exist to-day in most sizeable towns and cities draw a very high proportion of their clientele from youth. In many it is the exception to see a middle-aged couple, and often only a very small minority are over the age of about twenty-five. Organised large-scale dance-hall dancing is particularly a youth, and often an almost entirely youth, activity.

The following is an account of an evening in one of the large dance-halls in London:

8.15 p.m. Underground dance-hall. Area 50 yards by 30 yards. Tables and chairs along the two longest sides and behind them a raised section where dinner is served. Amongst the tables and chairs at each side are two parallel lines of five stone pillars. This leaves an actual dancing space of about 30 yards by 15 yards.

At the far end away from the entrance is a raised platform upon which an eight-piece band plays.

The colour scheme here is good—principal colour being red, with a secondary colour of fawn. Everything blends well. Predominant colour of the girls' clothes is also red.

A large fan is continually revolving in the middle of the ceiling.

There are about a hundred and fifty people here at present and a continual flow coming in. Only five people are over twenty-one. The majority, both male and female, are between seventeen and nineteen. Eight males in uniform and two females.

Twenty-five couples are dancing in a 'Jive' number. Seven couples are jitterbugging and the rest are doing an ordinary quickstep.

47

Six black males in Air Force uniform are dancing with white girls. The majority of them are 'jiving' whenever they get the opportunity.

About thirty males on their own are sitting around on the chairs; their main interest at the moment seems to be staring at the legs of the girls dancing.

During the pauses between the various dances both sexes lounge against the pillars; boys with their hands in their pockets 'ogling' their recent partners. In the majority of cases the youths seem to dance with different girls each time, or as many times as is possible, except for a few couples who came together. About 20 per cent of both males and females come on their own. Thirty per cent come as couples and 50 per cent in groups of two, three, or four—all of one sex.

Even at this comparatively early hour with a fan going, it is getting terribly stuffy, stale air combined with tobacco smoke.

About an equal number of the girls are wearing skirts and jumpers or blouses as are wearing frocks. Sports coats and flannels are worn in nearly every case by the males.

In the slow waltz now in progress the lights have been dimmed, and partners seen to be clasping each other as tight and as close as is possible. After having danced, about half walk away as pairs—arms interlocked—and half just leave the floor single. The males in no case see their partners to their chairs, etc., but just leave them in the middle of the floor and walk off to their own place.

With the younger girls, seventeen to eighteen, there seems to be great competition to dance with the Blacks, the reason being, I should imagine, their superb sense of rhythm and their natural ease of keeping in time with the music. There is not the slightest suggestion of colour distinction.

Very little talking going on considering the number of people here, except where a male is sitting a dance out with a girl. All the interest is centred around the dancing. On many faces there is a look of utter concentration, faces set and determined looking.

As soon as the band begins to play couples make their way on to the floor. Not the slightest reticence is shown by the males—if they want to dance they walk casually around the

48

edge of the floor looking at every girl until they find one of their choosing; they then walk up to the one of their choice and just tap her on the hand or shoulder. The 'tapped' one, then, without a word, rises, and they go on to the floor and dance, holding each other as if they had known each other for years. They come back the best of pals, sit down and become engrossed in conversation with each other.

No male was observed being refused a dance by any girl—they seem only too pleased at the opportunity to dance with anyone.

Most of the people here are of the working class. Only one or two 'Dago' or 'Spiv' types are present. They are dressed in their own, or rather the American, singular style—i.e. cut back collar with large knotted tie; 'Boston Slash Back' hair cut; and a 'house coat' style of jacket usually in a light fawn with brown flannels to match.

Two girls only are wearing slacks, and only four have their hair 'done up'. In the latter case they are usually an older and more sophisticated type of girl.

As time goes on fewer and fewer people remain on their own. Most have paired or grouped off quite successfully. The only ones still on their own are the girls of a not so attractive appearance, and some males who have not so far done any dancing.

These Blacks are certainly dancers in the truest sense of the word. The look on their faces as they 'jive' is a revelation. They are the picture of blissful joy and of utter contentment. Smiling most generally all the while and occasionally letting out a whoop or a yell.

About fifty girls are sitting and standing around the edge of the floor. They are waiting for prospective partners to ask them to dance. The number of males not dancing is about the same. When a girl's partner is not to her choice she has a most bored and sullen look on her face, and whilst dancing it changes to one of resignation and painful martyrdom.

Many of the girls seem to go through the whole evening without really enjoying themselves. They just seem to be awaiting their 'Prince Charming' to come along.

There are now about five middle-aged upper working class

couples here. They keep very much to themselves—they have not come together.

One youth here, of about twenty, seems either very shy or else very bored. He came in with a friend who has now found a girl. He is on his own at the moment. At first he was sitting on a chair just watching the dancing. After about 15 minutes he turned to a girl sitting near him and spoke about half a dozen words to her, smiled and then continued his 'just looking'. After another 15 minutes he stood up and wandered up and down the hall, hands in pockets, smiling rather vacantly and insipidly. He has just crossed over to the other side of the hall where he has seen some other friends, one male and two females. He is quite engrossed in conversation with them. After a while he dances with one of the girls and then continues to keep her as partner for the rest of the evening. He soon reveals himself as a Jive and Jitterbug fanatic.

Three youths of a 'Spiv' type have sauntered in. They are all wearing grey pin-striped flannels and the 'house coat' type of jacket. Two of them are wearing white shirts with a vivid Paisley tie, whilst the other is in a brilliant open-necked sports shirt. All these have carefully cared-for hair—long, with artificial waves, and a heavily greased 'Boston slash back' in two cases.

After almost an hour these three are still lounging up against the same pillar, just talking amongst themselves. Coats undone and hands in their pockets they are smoking continually and conversing amongst themselves or just staring on to the floor at the dancers.

9.15 p.m. Several couples sitting and caressing each other whilst many are sitting and lounging with arms around each other's waists.

The single males coming in at the moment are of a slightly older age—eighteen, nineteen and twenty. They are dressed in the American film star style—zoot suits, with heavily padded shoulders and collar attached shirts with the large knotted tie, usually in a plain colour. They are in groups of three or four and keep together most of the time. They spend the majority of

50

the time swaggering up and down the gangway between the rows of chairs and tables.

There are about fifteen youths of ages eighteen, nineteen and twenty standing on their own at the entrance to the dance floor. Hands in pockets, they simply stare ahead of them. They do not move. In most cases they stay there for about half an hour and then, very gradually, infiltrate into the hall and after much preliminary overhauling, they take their pick of a partner and begin to dance.

Some of the girls after having sat for most of the evening, give up hope of being asked to dance, and begin to dance amongst themselves. These girls when dancing amongst themselves seem, in every case, to favour the 'trucking style', i.e. really a glorified walk around the edge of the floor side by side and clasping hands behind each other's back, and making not very dextrous movements of the feet vaguely suggestive of the rhythm of the music.

In a quick step the majority of the people on the floor do a 'jive'. They yell and throw themselves about. Their whole body shakes, but what seems a rather contradictory factor is that their faces betray none of their apparent enthusiasm such as previously mentioned in the case of the Blacks, who are the only ones who really *show* enjoyment.

Provision is made for set meals at tables put apart. Waiters are in attendance. Only two couples so far have taken advantage of this—the majority favour lemonade and sandwiches obtainable in a separate bar.

Two medical students of about nineteen years of age from the University College Hospital start to speak to me and ask me what I am doing.

They tell me that they do not particularly want to come here themselves so much, it's their girl friends who insist on them coming. 'I get a feeling of superiority whenever I come here', one of them tells me. 'Why? Well, just look around you. Ha! Ha! What do you thing?'

10.00 *p.m.* Anyone is allowed to mount the platform and 'do their bit', which usually amounts to singing very briefly into a

51

microphone. The lights go out and spot lights of gay colours flicker on and off. It seems the right environment so most couples clasp each other even tighter and dance or nearly walk near together.

This is just a rough shuffling of the feet, most of the attention being paid to the proximity of the upper part of the body to that of one's partner.

Then the lights go on and the apparent spell is broken.

The majority of the amateur singers are the Blacks. They just walk up to the leader of the band, tell him what they wish to sing, and within a few moments they are in front of the microphone.

With well-known sentimental tunes like 'Bless You' and 'Sweetheart' most of the dancers join in and there is a constant volume of singing.

One insistent intruder of about twenty years of age is continually asking the band to accompany him in light classical numbers—'You are my heart's delight', 'Ah, sweet mystery of life', and a French song—this they are not willing to do. But after he has finished each one, he is greeted with much applause.

Funfair

Like the mass dance-hall, the funfair and amusement arcade is a large-town and city amenity. Quite near the dance-hall described above there are several funfairs, typical of many more. Here are descriptions of two of them:

1

The funfair has a floor space of about 40 feet deep by 25 feet wide. The walls are freshly painted a blue-green. The effect is slightly nautical. At the rear of the premises is a very miniature rifle range offering prizes for scores of 65 and over, six shots for a shilling. A notice proclaims that a score of 90 entitles the holder to a beautiful set of cutlery. But apart from this single recognition of marksmanship the prizes are cheap, consisting of vases, artificial flowers, paper carnival hats, tin whistles and lead pencils. Around the walls and down the centre are rows of 'pin tables', various machines all involving the use of a small metal ball, a 'Punch Bag' ('Punch your weight'), and an automatic fortune teller named 'Sylvia the Gypsy Queen'— this was a particularly expensive-looking piece of mechanism. A wizened old man in a white coat tended the rifle range, and a young man with a limp carried a leather bag over his shoulder, from which he changed the silver coins of the players for the pennies to be fed to the waiting machines.

When the investigator entered, the place was deserted except for the staff and one undersized boy, possibly fifteen years of age. He looked clean, intelligent but apathetic. He wore a dark double-breasted jacket, much too large for him; and long grey trousers which seemed to rest in folds on the top of his well polished army type boots. He stood in front of a pin table offering a prize for a score of '11,500 or over'. His attitude was of mild interest in the game. From time to time he tried to coax the metal ball into a particular hole by jarring the table with a sharp jab delivered by the ball of his hand. (This is strictly against the rules.) At the end of three games at a penny per game, he turned as he heard a coin drop into an adjacent machine. It was called 'The Novelty Merchantman', and the coin had set in motion a small derrick on the deck of a model ship; the derrick moved a grab which poised, swooped, picked up a box of ten Players cigarettes and then dropped them neatly into a large hole connected by a chute to a place accessible to the winner. The player was the limping member of the staff. He retrieved and pocketed the cigarettes, looked at the boy as though to say 'That's the way to do it', and moved away.

The boy proceeded to lose three more pennies striving for an elusive packet of twenty Players, then, stuffing his hands deep into his trousers pockets, he walked slowly round the rows of pin tables and wandered out into the road. On the pavement he looked first left then right, paused a moment, and finally moved off. After every few steps he kicked at an imaginary object.

This is a larger establishment, walls and fittings are painted in cream, red and black. In addition to the inevitable pin tables and rifle range, there is a live fortune teller called 'Yvonne' who occupied a booth covered with mystical and astrological symbols. A giant panatrope blares forth popular tunes. Hung around the walls are 'hand-painted' pictures depicting human and animal oddities each with an explanatory card beneath. A portrait of a gentleman in a toga fondling a horse carries the caption 'Caligula, a Roman Emperor, made his horse a Consul'. A giant of a man is revealed as 'Daniel Lambert of U.S.A. who weighed fifty-two stones and eleven pounds'. A cow with two udders, one on her back 'gave milk from both'. And a strange looking bearded little man was 'Little Peter of Petersburg who though less than three feet tall had ten wives and thirty-seven children'.

About twenty people were scattered around the tables, playing, or watching others at play. Two raincoated lads of sixteen watched a man throwing darts. They stood quietly, hands in pockets, until the man moved over to a pin table and then they followed him and watched again. After a few minutes one of the boys produced a penny and began to play himself. The other boy transferred his attention from the man to his friend, but said nothing. He leaned against the pin table and watched. At another table stood a young man about twenty years old and five feet tall. He was dark and good looking with well-greased hair and fashionable side burns, he wore a navy blue overcoat of good material draped in 'the American manner' and extending almost to his calves. The face was expressionless as he played, and his hands soft looking with over long black-rimmed finger nails. Penny after penny was inserted into the machine and ball after ball shot round the table and disappeared. Two young girls came in arm in arm, giggling and whispering together. They each wore thin summer overcoats over print dresses. Their faces were heavily and inexpertly made up, one sported a pair of long earrings; as they brushed past the young man at the pin table he turned his head and looked them over appraisingly. They caught his glance—and arched. The dark young man turned back to the pin table and inserted another penny.

A few minutes later the investigator heard voices in argument coming from the far side of the hall. He crossed over and saw an attendant in a white coat pointing vigorously to a notice nailed to the wall and saying 'Come on now, out you go'. The notice read 'Girls under the age of eighteen will not be admitted to this establishment. This is a POLICE LAW and must be enforced'. The girl with the earrings took her friend by the arm and said, 'Come on Millie, what do yer expect from dese lousy bastards', but Millie was not to be appeased, 'What I wan' ter know is 'ow do you know I'm not eighteen'. The attendant took her free arm and began to lead her out saying, 'I know, see, so be a good girl and git'. The man and the two girls walked to the exit where they stood for a few minutes talking in low voices, the man earnest and apologetic, the girls still a trifle upset. Finally, with a toss of her head, Millie said to her friend, 'Well, come on, what are we waitin' for'. And both the girls walked off in the direction of Oxford Street. Back in the Fun Fair the dark young man was still shooting little balls at holes.

These are some of the leisure-pleasure amenities available for city youth. According to the last census eight out of ten young people live in towns, and it is generally agreed that the delinquency problem is mainly a townee problem. So, although these typify the *sort* of activity which, to a greater or lesser extent, occupies a great deal of the leisure time of a great many young people, let us now take a more intimate look at the daily life of a city child.

V

DELINQUENT IN THE MAKING?

Here we examine more closely the early start of what may, or may not, develop from the background of drift into a delinquent career. This is, in a way, the familiar textbook history of negligent parents, lack of moral background, absence of father, etc. etc. It differs from most textbook case histories in the important respect that the observer herself is relatively sympathetic with the viewpoint of the adults involved, is inclined only to evaluate their behaviour in relation to its effect on the child, and is on naturally friendly terms with the household. She is 'close to the racket' herself in some ways. In other words her acknowledged bias runs in the opposite direction to the acknowledged bias of most who study or report such subjects. No one can be entirely without bias in the overall observation of human behaviour, and the bias of the moralist will, other things being equal, render his observations just as selective as those of the amoralist. This remains true until controls are applied which only become useful in the later stages of research, when a fully documented hypothesis is being put to the final scientific test.

The person who recorded this history at M-O's request, has herself earned money in marginal and near-crime ways. She is a teetotaller. Her taste in dress is neat, smart and quiet, and she wears little make-up. Her centres of interest are vigorously and broadly humanitarian, and equally vigorously anti-authoritarian. Each of these biases and predilections could, perhaps, be detected from the emphases, and the slurs, apparent in this description. So, equally, can the predilections of those responsible for writing down the more familiar case-history—of textbook on the one hand, and 'revelation' on the other. At this stage a less familiar bias is useful in balancing the picture. She writes :

JIMMY

The flat opposite to mine is occupied by a Cockney family consisting of a man about forty-five to fifty years old, who appears to be a builder's labourer or demolition worker; a woman, forty-five to fifty, with platinum blonde, waved hair, but not 'flashy' otherwise, just decently dressed; a young woman, known as 'Peg', about thirty, very slim, rather attractive, but not 'flashy', no make up and usually rather dirty; and a little boy, Jimmy, aged eight, who is Peg's son. I have never been told the actual relationship of these people, but have gathered from remarks of their own that 'Uncle Bob', the man, is the father of Peg, but is not married to the blonde woman, who presumably lives with him.

Jimmy calls the blonde 'Connie', the man 'Uncle Bob', and Peg 'Mummy'. Alternatively, the blonde may be the mother of Peg and Uncle Bob the outsider. There is no man who could 'fit-in' as Jimmy's father, and neighbours say that Peg and her husband are separated and that Peg has a flat on her own not far away and spends her time between the two.

All the adults are fond of drink and the two women seem to spend most of their time in local pubs. During the war, Jimmy was evacuated and I saw very little of him. Only when the war finished did he return to live at the flat opposite. During the time he was away, Peg spent most of her days and nights in the pubs and there was an American soldier who used to visit her fairly frequently. He drove a large truck and it used to be parked for hours outside the house, though never all night. Peg was obviously not a prostitute—just a good-time girl, who appeared to care little for anything but drink. She is not interested in dress, or make-up, just dresses in a plain coat or costume, no stockings, court shoes, no hat, wears her hair in a straight, long bob. She gives the impression she has just got out of bed, put on dress, shoes and coat, without much face-washing and hair-combing and hurried off to the 'pub'. She and the blonde woman frequently leave the flat about 11 o'clock in the morning and I have often seen Peg returning about 3 p.m., very drunk, though she always walks well and only shows it by her speech.

At night, I have often seen Uncle Bob and the blonde returning from the pub, she always more drunk than he, and occasionally there are rows late at night—screams and shouts and sounds of fighting.

During the war I very rarely saw the blonde, and Uncle Bob, once when slightly drunk, told me that his 'old woman' spent all her time in the pubs and the shelter (a Tube station) and would not come home at all. He said: 'I give her four quid a week to spend all her time in the shelter.' This was, of course, during the raids and later during the flying-bomb period.

Although both women spend a lot of time away from the flat and do so much drinking, they, or possibly the blonde, keep the flat quite clean. At least, the hall and one bedroom which I have seen were quite clean and quite well furnished. This, then, is the background of Jimmy.

I first became aware of Jimmy as a 'problem child' soon after he returned from evacuation. He naturally made quite a lot of noise, banging in and out of the flat and up and down stairs, and he used to bring several other children to play on the stairs. They used to knock on my door and then hide and I presume they did this to the other tenants. I used to have a card with my name pinned on my door, but they tore this off regularly, so I finally stopped putting one up there. I did not mind these small annoyances, however, and Jimmy did not upset me in any other way, but I began to hear remarks made by the caretaker of the flats and tenants which indicated that Jimmy was causing quite a lot of trouble.

I occasionally heard rows on the landing caused by people coming to complain to Jimmy's family of him breaking down garden gates and stealing things. Uncle Bob usually dealt with these complaints and he seemed to take the line that it 'was always *his* kid who was to blame and what about young Johnny so-and-so?' etc. But he usually ended up by accepting the evidence against Jimmy and later I would hear indications of questioning Jimmy and threatening him and occasionally thrashing him. There was one occasion when I saw a policeman ride up on a bicycle, come up to the flat opposite and knock on the door. I listened, and when the door opened he said: 'Are you the mother of Jimmy—?' Peg's voice answered : 'Yes', and then he said : 'I'm afraid your son is in a spot of trouble again.' He then went inside and I heard no more. I began to gather from happenings of this kind that Jimmy was causing more trouble than the average child of eight years of age.

I have never heard the full story, although I have had several conversations with Uncle Bob about Jimmy. But he has not told the whole truth, perhaps naturally, and his remarks are very disjointed. I gathered that Jimmy constantly played truant from school and it was during the day, in the company of other kids, that most of his 'crimes' were committed. But he appears to have done it more often than others and to be most to blame. On one occasion he stole two pet rabbits from a garden and hid them in a bombed-out building, presumably intending to feed them and keep them for himself. It seems that every effort was made to get him to school (possibly after pressure from the police and school-inspectors), because on some occasions Peg took him herself to the school in the morning, and I was told that he had 'even climbed over the wall to get out again'.

The final 'crime' and one I heard most about was as follows: In the flat below the family lives an old lady, a churchwoman I gather. She came home one day to find she had forgotten her key, and she asked Jimmy to climb through her scullery window, (her flat is on the ground floor), and let her in. Some weeks after this she found that her handbag had been rifled and money and ration cards stolen during her absence. She apparently knew that it was Jimmy who had again climbed through the scullery window, this time without being asked! I don't know how it was proved, but she made a scene on the landing about it and eventually went to the police. She evidently hated Jimmy and his family because she said they were a nuisance to all the other tenants and that Jimmy was a bad, wicked boy in the neighbourhood and that he ought to be sent away. She had her wish— he was!

It appears that this was his third time at the Children's Court and it was decided to send him to a Home for a trial period of three weeks. During this three weeks, on the very day his mother and the blonde went to visit him, he escaped with another boy and came to London without any money. It appears that when the two women arrived at the Home, Jimmy was sent for and it was only then discovered that he had gone; this was at 4 o'clock in the afternoon. The women came back and it is significant that at 9 o'clock Jimmy and his friend arrived *at the pub,* not at home, to find his mother. They were brought home and Uncle Bob went and told the police and the next day they were sent back.

He had refused to tell how they got to London but said he was quite happy at the Home and had only come home for a holiday; he was quite willing to go back again. Apparently this escapade caused the authorities to decide he must stay longer than three weeks, because he has not returned home since.

The only person who has really tried to care for Jimmy is Uncle Bob, and most of the rows when they have been drunk seem to be between the two women as to who should look after Jimmy, Uncle Bob accusing them both of spending all their time drinking and neglecting the kid.

They have not been actually unkind to him; probably in the sense of money to spend and freedom to go to the pictures, he has been spoiled; but they have never been there to give him his meals or let him in the flat. I have heard him knocking for hours at intervals during the day and being unable to get in.

On one occasion I saw him from my window, standing in the rain outside the flats at dinner-time. I asked him was his mother not in and he said: 'No— I want my dinner.' I said: 'Well, you can't play outside on a day like this, will you come in with me?' He did so. He stayed from 12.30 till 3 and had some dinner with me. He said that he had been to school in the morning but would not go back in the afternoon. He also said: 'I know my Mummy will be in the 'York' or the 'King's Head', but she'll be mad with me if I go looking for her.'

I did not want to question him because I don't want to encourage a child to talk about his family or home, but I said, 'Why don't you have your dinner at school with the other kids?' He said: 'Mummy doesn't want me to, but I think I am going to next week.'

During the time he was with me he behaved very well. He

60

was, like a child, interested in various ornaments and things he saw about the flat, but he did not touch anything without asking my permission and he spoke nicely, in a simple, innocent sort of way and had quite good manners.

This was the only occasion I asked him into my home, though probably if I had looked for him, there would have been many times when he was lonely and cold and would have been glad to come in. But although I was sorry for the kid and really liked him, I was afraid of causing trouble with the family. I know that people of that kind resent any sort of interference and the implication that others know that the child is neglected. On this occasion, when he heard somebody entering the flat opposite, he said : 'That will be Mummy', and rushed over there. It *was* Peg and she was a bit drunk. A short time afterwards I heard him crying and her shouting and sounds of him being chased and slapped. I don't know whether this was because he had not gone back to school or because he had accepted my hospitality. I was very sorry if I was to blame but could, of course, say or do nothing.

They did not change in their attitude to me, however, and I once seized the opportunity of saying that I liked Jimmy and had enjoyed his company and that I thought him a nice, simple, well-behaved little boy. They seemed pleased and nothing further was said. I really do think that he is a bright, open, intelligent, 'simple' (as opposed to 'complicated') child, with an instinct for adventure and innocent mischief. He has simply 'gone wrong' through a longing for company and affection and through being left alone without his energy and interests being directed into proper channels.

I don't know how long he was evacuated, nor where—he may have got his good manners and nice way of speaking whilst away. I don't mean his accent was good—he speaks like any London kid, but he speaks openly and innocently—not furtive or sly, nor affected, as some quite young children do. I do not think that he would have stolen anything from me, nor annoyed me as he apparently did other tenants, because he knew I was his friend and 'on his side'.

After I had been in my flat some months, I began to give him chocolate and chewing-gum which I got from Americans and I would have a few words with him when we met. After that he never knocked at my door and ran away as he had done at first, not because I bribed him, but because he liked me and felt I was not criticising him, nor complaining of his behaviour as the others did. I think that the pranks he played and the small thefts he made were chiefly on the people he felt to be his enemies—the old woman downstairs and the caretaker, who were always complaining of the noise he made, etc. I think it is fairly likely his family talk to school authorities, magistrates, etc., as if they did everything possible for him and punished him severely for his 'crimes'. (They certainly did 'punish' him, though not very severely.) They would not, of course, admit that the two women spent their time in pubs and that Jimmy is left far too much alone to roam the streets. I don't know if the various authorities know anything of the truth. But to me Jimmy is not at all a 'problem child', and given love and affection, and a cheerful home and the feeling of being wanted and cared for, he would be a perfectly normal, likeable little boy.

★   ★   ★

So much for Jimmy, seen through the wall of the next room. He is, in a sense, a pawn—perhaps a rather pathetic pawn—of circumstance. Others operate at a less 'accidental' level, at least in the outward meaning of that word. One feels, writing on this subject, how inadequate the terms and definitions are, how little the main descriptive terms of such subjects are agreed— even among experts, who indeed tend to confuse them. But let us hear from another 'type'—if it is safe to call him that.

VI

DELINQUENT MADE

'His Next Course is Bread and Water'

RECAPTURED to-day after his third escape from Dartmoor-Prison, twenty-three-year-old Borstal trainee, —— ——, of Kidder-minster, is to-night in the punishment block on low diet.

Bread and water, however, should not worry ——, for he has admitted that last night, during his brief spell of freedom, he consumed at least 4 lb. of roast pork, 9 lb. of biscuits and 2 lb. of marmalade.

To-day police and warders found Bywaters in the piggeries on the prison farm with the remains of a piglet he had killed on the floor. The biscuits and marmalade, used to round off the repast, came from a 56 lb. box of biscuits and a 40 lb. case of marmalade that disappeared during the night from a naval victualling store nearby.'

(News Chronicle, 17th January 1947.)

'By stealing the child hopes for libidinal satisfaction, though in reality it proves ineffective, because the symbol of love has been mistaken for the evil thing. From earliest days libidinal satisfaction is associated with obtaining possession of things. In infancy it is milk, in later years toys and sweets; and even in adult life a drink, a box of chocolates, a cigarette or a good meal are the tokens of kindly feelings from one person to another. Food and other objects thus become symbols of affection. An adult thief . . . whom I have treated . . . had the habit of taking her morning tea from a baby's bottle . . .'

(JOHN BOWLBY, Forty-Four Juvenile Delinquents.)

'Spivs, it may be seen, live easy—for a time... Theirs is a sad little story, and a short little story. Ask a policeman—he knows.' (*Evening News,* 16th December 1946.)

The following extracts are from a long account of his life written by a young, very habitual, thief. This account is presented in deliberate contrast to the previous autobiographical extract. The boy shows no sign at all of feeling dogged by fate. For long periods his life of theft is successful, and he holds jobs successfully until he feels inclined to give them up. Unless we read very deeply between the lines, his account appears very much like a success-story.

Spiv? Psychotic? Social Menace? Affectionless Character? Whatever the docket, this is an indication of how it feels to be one.

Three extracts are given. The first concerns the boy's early memories of stealing sweets and 'pop' from shops. The second deals with his adolescent life during a long period of successful 'living-easy'; the third with the day he receives a Borstal sentence.

1. THE START

The first thing I did wrong was on a Sunday evening I was about 12 years old then, there were three of us my brother my cousin and me. We started to fool around behind an old warehouse and we found that one of the windows was partly open and gets in and sees typewriters big books and samples of toffy choclates biscits sweets corned beef sauce 'eat' until we was really full up then we started to search in the other rooms and we find cases full of watches, so we takes one each and searches in the other draws and find a box of stamps and a small box of money, so that was all we wanted for the time being so we gets out the same way as we got in, and we makes our way for the cafe and we spends five shillings of our money by 9 o'clock and then its time to go home so we counts the money we have got left and divide it between us and we have twelve and three-pence each.

I hides the money on the side of the path as I go up to the house and dad asks the usual question and sends us to bed and we put heads underneath the bedclothes and switches on the torches and looks at the watches until we falls off to sleep, and we spends the money quietly, and Thursday the three of us disides to break into the pop stores so we goes out soon after tea and quietly takes a sheet of tin off the side and goes in and switches on our torches and we see cases and cases of pop so we drinks as much as we can and then we sees tins of crisps so we gets stuck into them and goes into the ofice and ransacle the draws and we finds two bundles of candles and a bag of crisps through a door and we disides to take some cases of pop and tins of crisps so my brother goes homes and gets the big four wheal troly and we puts about six cases of pop and three tins of crisps and we takes them under the old castle ruins and lights the candles and we hides the cases and tins until tomorrow night.

We goes friday and saterday night to have a blow out, and on the Sunday we disides to go into the warhouse again so we goes in and we made a good haul and hid the stuff the same place as the pop and crisps and as we goes past the wearhouse we sees a light in there so I tells them to keep away it might be the police, and my cousin went over to look in the room a P.C. Woods puts his hand on his shoulder and says what do you know about it and he tells him and Matthew and me dashes off and waits about five minits and my cousin comes running up saying that we have got to go down to the wearhouse and he says that if we go down he will let us off so we goes down for my cousins sake and the copper asks us to go to his house to clear things up so we goes to his house and he asks us our names and addresses, so I says to him I wont tell you, so my cousin tells him his address and he locks the door and goes of to find his father.

While he is gone we opens the window and dashes of to our hideout under the castle, and we hides there for a week and our food and stuff runs out so we disides to break into the grocers and on our way we sees dad coming up the road and we try to make a bunk but dad soon catches us and he takes us home and he sends my other brother to fetch the copper.

We find something to eat by the time he came and he asks us the questions in the house, and tells dad that we have got to attend court on Friday and when he had gone dad got me in the corner and belted hell out of me, and the same happened to my brother, and when we asked my cousin what happened to him and he says he did not get a hideing, because he was only led into it so we gave him a hideing.

On Friday we goes to court in front of D— and he sentences me and my brother to twelve months probation and a fine of ten shillings each, and my cousin gets six months probation when he ought to get three years aprove school.

2. SUCCESS

(This boy worked as a miner, mate to one of his relatives, for seven months; then decided to go to London. We take up the narrative in London.)

A week later I starts to look for a job and I gets one in the same place as my brother works, and the first thing he puts me on is sweeping up and he tells me to springcle water on the floor to stop the dust from rising, so instead of sprinkling it, I pored the whole bocket on the floor and my brother comes to me and sayd you will get the sack for that, so I says I dont care so I starts to mop it up before the foreman comes, and as I finnishes it the foreman comes up to me and says thanks sony thats the best thing I have seen done since I have come here, and he says he will see me alright so I got well in with him from the start he then put me on a driller and learns me the delicate art of it, which I can say that in a week I was as good as anyone and so I get on.

He then puts me on a miller which I soon learn to use, and then he puts me on the lathe which is the best job of the lot, but after four months of it, I say well I have a little holiday so I asks for my cards which he refuses to give me he says you stay on and I will give you a rise, but I refused it and he asks my brother to try and get me to stay, and I was more determined than ever to have my cards, so he gives in and gives me a good reference, and three shillings and he says if you want your job back you can have it, and I say good afternoon to him.

I makes my way to the fair ground, and see nobody there so I disides to go to the pictures and on my way there I see a girl I knew by sight so I says good afternoon, and she replies, so we gets chatting and I asks her will she come to the pictures with me and she say its my half day off so I takes her to the pictures and we stays in there till half past severn, and then we catches a bus to the fair and we enjoy ourselves till about eleven o'clock then we go for a walk through the woods and I reaches home about half past twelve and tip toes quietly to the dining room and have my supper and takes my shoes of and goes quietly to bed and I find that my brother has not come in yet, but I falls of to sleep before he comes in.

And in the morning my antie wakes me and wants to know what time I want to get up so I says about ten o'clock and then I falls off to sleep, and wakesup at quarter to ten by my watch so I gets up and have a bath and togs up in my evening clothes, and goes for a walk as I passes a big house I sees two cars coming down the drive, and they had cases of luggage straped to the back, so I puts two and two together and says to myself that, there wont be anybody in the house and I'll be able to break in.

I reaches the front door I find that I am correct because there was two envelopes on the ledge and I opens one, and there eight and fourpence for the milkman and a note saying not to put any milk down for five days, and one for the baker but there was only one and elevenpence in with the same note, so I goes round the back and breaks the lavatory window and gets in that way, and I picks up two wrist watches, a gold edge cigarette case and a cigarette lighter and nine pounds and three pence in the rent book and I then break the gas-meter open and get about two pounds out of it so I did not do to bad altogether.

I then goes home and have my dinner and pays my antie twelve shillings from the money I had for my wages. After dinner I jumps on the bus and goes shopping to see what I could buy with the money. I buys a smart trilby and a silk neckerchief and a pair of furlined gloves, then I starts to make my way to the Odeon cinema and I goes to a shop to get some cigarettes and sweets, so I drops in the arcade and has a go at the machines, and gets so interested that I do not notice the time, and then I look up I find it is too late to go to the pictures.

So I slips over to the cafe to have a snak and comes out half an hour later to have another go at the machines, and in the end I gets the nack how to use them and I keeps on winning the prizes.

At severn o'clock I catches the K — — — bus and jumps off at the fair to meet my girl and have another nights fun at the fair and have the same walk along the wood about severn o'clock, two days later the fair goes and I do not know what to do in the evenings, but has luck would have it I saw another fair going to W . . . and it would be going in full swing so I went to call up my mate on Friday evening and told him to bring his girl with him, so that the four of us could have a good time at the fair.

The first thing we went on was the dodge-ems and we was on them for about two hours, banging one another and cutting each other in to the side and than we went on the big lizzy which is just like a swinging boat only much larger and was covered in, it starts of quietly and as it gains speed you are practikly looking strait at the ground, and the girls started to hang on us saying that they felt sick, so after a couple of minits it dies down and I told them to stay in and we'll get of before it starts again, so I gives the driver a shilling and gives im the nod to start of and away we go before the girls knew where they were, and Joyce held on to me like a leach, and kept on saying I will finnish with you, and I says right I can soon pick up another and she was the first to get off, and she would not speak to me for half an hour, so I jumps back on to the dodge-ems and she looks on until they have finnished and then I haves pity and calls her on and she comes on and makes up for it.

Two weeks latter I find that all I have got is ten shilling, and so I goes round looking for a job and gets one at the . . . Co. at a pound per week. So on the monday I goes there and starts work, and at the end of two months I packs that in and gets a job in a wireless, electrical and cycle shop at . . . and I only lasts there for two months. I gets the sack on suspicion of taking old wireless sets and cycle parts etc.,

I then gets a job at an electrical factory and I was put on peace work the first week I was there and I was coming home with thirty five shillings a week, I was there I think it was four months until I got the sack for breaking two cutters and I came home with three pounds fifteen for eleven days which was pretty good.

Then I disides to have anothers weeks rest, so I breaks into two cafes and gets about twenty pounds worth of stuff from there and we goes and sells it to a fellow in a small canteen for ten pounds and me and Johnny has five pounds and about thirty shillings each from the tills so Johnny gets his cards from work, and we goes up town together and goes into regents park zoo to spend a day and we comes back in the bus and jumps of about half way to have a nice walk home.

On our way, we pass a garage, and see the fellow put some money in a till and walks outside, so we goes through the back door and carries the till out to the fields, we then opens it and find its practickly full of mony there was seventy two pounds in notes about fourteen to fifteen pounds in silver and copper.

So we dumps the till and goes of home and pack a few belongings and gets toged up, and we catches the morning train from Padington to Newport, and from Newport we catches a bus to Barry and we find cheap lodgings which cost us twelve shillings per day and day after day we goes on to the island and haves the best time you could wish, and we picks up two smashing bits of stuff, and well what else could you ask for.

Just after three weeks of it we find that funds are running low, so we packs our bags and make our way home, and then we thinks of looking for a job and me and Johnny gets a job at a motorcycle garage, and we gets on pretty well, we learns how to ride the motor bikes and we quietly takes parts of a good motor cycle and fits them back again at home until we have got the whole of the bike and we gets it to go, and we runs it around the fields until we are pretty good experts at the game, and a couple of days after that I gets the sack.

So I starts to look for work again and I gets a job at a signmakers at thirty shillings a week so I disides not to lose this job I'll try to keep it, after I have been there a week, he says to me that I will have to work in August week so I tells him that I will not I would rather have my cards.

3. FAILURE

(There are several more jobs, and several more 'jobs' success-fully completed before the (temporary?) end of the story in a Borstal sentence.)

I get two pounds a week at the tomato nurseries, and after a month of it I packs it up and starts on the job of breaking into houses, and everything goes smoothly for a month, and as I was coming out of a house a paper boy sees me, and give my description to the cops, and that night as I was coming from the fair, four men came up to me and asks me could I see them alone and I says yes soon as I takes my girl home and they says alright but they will come behind you.

So I took my girl home and goes back to those men and they says that they are police officers and they have had my descrip-tion for breaking into a house and they tried to search me only I would not have it and of course they said come along for further enquirys and they grabed hold of me by the scruff of the neck and put me in the car that they had waiting and they said we have these three charges against you for house-breaking and they took me from there to H . . . and of course I was under a false name of R . . . S . . .

Next morning they fetched in my breakfast and about half past ten the officer asked me did I want any cigarettes and I said I have got some in my property and would you please get them for me, and he comes back five minutes later with my cigarettes and matches and he asks me to go into his office and he asks me for my finger prints and I refuse to let him take them, so he talks to me quietly and he says that I am forced to, so I lets him take my finger prints, and I says to myself its all up now, they will soon know my real name because I have had my finger prints taken before.

So to save them the bother of looking me up I tells them my right name and he thanks me and says you may smoke so I stays there until Monday and they takes me up to court, and they remands me for the sessions in two months time, but I did not do too bad at the scrubs I was getting a visit every week, and brought a parcel with her every time, and dad gets me a solicitor to help me at the court.

So when I goes to court I asks one of the officers could he get me some cigarettes so he says yes and stops the police van and gets me a tin of cigarettes, he said I will need them before the days out, so one of the fellows that I made up with at the scrubs is practically broke, so I gives him some of the cigarettes, and when we reach there, we were put in the same cell, and I asks the officers could we have some books and chocolate, and he says, yes, so I gives him orders and he gets them for me.

So we were smoking, reading and chewing until half past twelve when the officer came round and asks us do we want to buy a dinner, so I buys two dinners, the other one for my mate.

At two o'clock the officer calls my mates name to go up to court and five minutes I goes up the next court, and the solicitor says a lot of rubbish about me going strate and I will go back home to my parents and says all this lad needs is good up-bringing, and strict training, so the judge has a little conference with the rest, and turns around to me and says, well lad we agree to what you want and what you will have and give you another chance to make good, (so I says to myself I have done it again) therefore I sentence you to a Borstal Institution for three years (and then my face drops).

★　　　★　　　★

So far we have seen the individual rather than his full unit, the family, to which so many experts directly attribute all the repercussions of criminality. It is time we dipped into our file of documents at this family-party level, seen slightly wider than the individual subjective view of one interested party . . .

VII

FAMILY I

Let us agree, then, that all young delinquents are not brought to book; that, say, one in five are. With six to the thousand found guilty, this would mean that about thirty to the thousand actually commit these serious or, more technically, these indictable offences.

This means that every year some 970 children in every thousand never commit offences at all. It also means that the great majority of our children reach man's estate without having once committed an offence against the laws of their country —or at most have fallen from grace only once or twice; and many of these because they fell victims to the sort of circumstances which set some unexpected temptation in their way rather than because there happened to be in their make-up an extra measure of original sin.'

(*The Juvenile Courts*, F. F. GILES, Allen & Unwin, 1946.)

A Mass-Observation investigator, attending a dance of a well-known open-air youth organisation of which he is a member, casually asked all those he conversed with during the evening a few informal questions about their habits in regard to certain 'illegal' actions. He reported thus:

'The impression gained after asking people of the things they could remember having stolen was that the majority of people of all ages "took things" from their place of occupation and that they did not really consider this stealing. "But everybody does it", one said. "A person who makes nails never buys any", said another.

72

'Although nobody spontaneously mentioned the fact, when questioned, as to whether they had travelled on the railway without paying the proper fare, all admitted doing so and did not regard it as being relevant as "law-breaking". Out of 25 persons asked if they had ever paid less than the correct fare, 23 answered "Yes" and 2 "No".'

Most people, as we have earlier seen, are 'delinquent' in a technical sense, acquiring at times some object to which they are not legally entitled. The number of towels stolen from the Great Western Railway alone in the last year in which towels, *ad lib,* were available to steal, was over six times as great as the total number of people convicted of larceny in the whole country.

As Mr. A. E. Jones [1] puts it: 'As a general proposition it is incontestable that first and foremost as a deterrent to anti-social conduct comes the strength of public opinion.'

Mr. Jones contrasts the deterrent effect of neighbours' opinions in a city slum, in a village and in a middle class suburb. At least as important a factor in this respect, however, as the environment in which the 'delinquent' *lives,* is the place from which he steals, or in which he does his 'delinquent' act. In a lavatory he steals his towel and secretes it on his person or in his bag, behind a locked door. So lavatories suffer particularly from the latent delinquency in nearly all of us.

A great deal is written about the broken home, the lack of parental interest and love, as factors predisposing children towards delinquency. That picture is reasonably familar, and need not be re-drawn here. Rather less familiar is the non-broken home, where there is plenty, or too much, of affection, but where values and environment take delinquency in their stride as part and parcel of normal behaviour.

Here is one such home, described by a sympathetic neighbour who has studied it for years.

THE PLACE

Large house, four or five storey, in central district—well-furnished, that is with fairly expensive modern furniture, good

[1] *Juvenile Delinquency and the Law* (Pelican Books, 1946).

carpets, mirrors, etc., grouped together in various rooms with no background or features. The house, apart from times when party is ensuing and beer and spirit bottles and glasses are littering the place, is devoid of personality like a furniture showroom.

FATHER

Father is a bookmaker. Round and ruddy type—well-established at dog-meetings, horse-racing; also employs men who run street-books. *Probably* started to make his book on proceeds of his wife's shop-liftings. Seems almost oblivious of son's existence apart from times when son has parties in the house, but usually these occur when he happens to be away for a two- or three-day meeting.

MOTHER

Mother used to be a shop-lifter. Aged forty, appears younger, thirtyish, smart, well-dressed, almost suburban in appearance—very strong Cockney accent; spends most evenings in local pubs with one or other of her many men friends—most of them acquaintances of her husband.

Has no conversation apart from clothes, cinema and who's been 'done' this week—'done' having two different meanings—to be 'done' by the boys, means to be 'beaten up' by fellow criminal types; to be 'done' by the 'bogeys', means to be arrested by the police or to be convicted and sent to prison.

Since she no longer has any necessity to indulge in crime actively, she works as receiver and is in this way in close contact with her old associates without opening herself to the greater risks of shop-lifting; her receiving is mostly wearing apparel, furs, model gowns, coats, lingerie, etc., proceeds of the others' shop-lifting. I have heard her referred to as 'the best hoister in the game'; she may have been to prison, but I have no knowledge of this. She has an overwhelming devotion towards and pride in her son—an only child. In actions she treats him like a small boy, brushes dust from his coat, straightens his tie, etc., but in conversation he is treated as an equal—he calls her by her Christian name and is generally quite familiar with her men friends.

74

Jack, aged seventeen, no occupational training of any sort—has never had a job since he left school, which was at the earliest possible time. His parents in spite of financial status, never at any period (so far as could be observed), had any ambition of allowing him to be educated further than the law insisted.

His clothes are made for him by an expensive West End tailor, and he also wears handmade shoes. His mother meets these bills and invites more. 'About time you got yourself some new clobber, ain't it, Jack?' she has said almost every time I have met her. In spite of his almost dandyish appearance he has no respect for these clothes and is quite frequently involved in typical West End 'rough and tumbles' in which bottles, chairs and even knives are used.

His days are spent lounging about the West End back streets with the 'boys', evenings in pubs and cheap West End clubs—billiard saloons and pin-table saloons (the latter are not over-popular). In the early hours he may be seen almost every morning lolling at a table in a café with some of the 'boys'. They play 'poker-dice' at the tables—sometimes on the floor under the tables—in the gents' toilet—and sometimes in the back streets.

They sell hot goods to each other—sometimes they go to lesser-known night clubs in a body. Quite often there are scrimmages in the café, in which case if one of their pals is involved, they will all start in. Should it be a friend who is drunk and is deliberately picking a quarrel, they try to get him out and send or take him home. If, as may happen, the fight has nothing to do with them, there are certain members of the fraternity who will gather into the crowd collected round the fight and pick pockets, dip handbags, etc. I have never known Jack to pick pockets but he is part of the atmosphere—' 'ow much d'yer get? two nickels? a s—b . . . chicken-feed!'

Despite his background, and despite his habits, Jack has never been in the hands of the police, so far as can be ascertained (and there is no reason to suppose he would hesitate to admit it if he had).

★　　　★　　　★

In the following section we present, in much more detail, the family background of some other children who have *not* followed in their parents' footsteps. This account outlines the history of a large family, all of whom, in the generation now parents, are 'delinquent' to some degree. Yet the children, brought up during the war, apparently show no signs of delinquency.

This history is written by a personal friend who has been intimately acquainted with the family for several years. It is given at some length for two reasons. Firstly, it is an example, to all appearances at least, of a perfectly *happy* family whose opposition to the laws and orders of society has become traditional in the second generation. They are consequently not affected by the scruples, conscience, anxiety, etc., of those brought up to consider 'crime' as a cause of shame. This aspect of the 'happy delinquent' is one to which attention is seldom drawn.

Secondly, the story demonstrates particularly well the co-existence of a quite coherent moral code, strong affections and conventionally praiseworthy family ties, with a life of large-scale 'fiddling' and other legal misdemeanours and crimes.

VIII

FAMILY 2

A large amount of the law-breaking which swells the records of our juvenile courts (and of the adult courts?) is an evidence not of youthful depravity, not even of psychopathic conditions, but of the fact that we are applying to a primitive people the rather arbitrary laws of a highly sophisticated era.'

(Margery Fry.)

THE FAMILY

There was Mum, the Old Man, and seven children—four sons and three daughters. They were an ordinary Cockney family, but had a rather mixed ancestry and had not always been 'common'. Mum often told me that her mother was a 'lady', and some years afterwards this was confirmed by a chance acquaintance of mine who had known Mum's family.

MUM

In any case Mum only vaguely remembered living in a big house on Barton Hill and her upbringing after that appears to have been very ramshackle. She did not like to talk about it and I only have a rough idea of what happened to her before she married Harding. I know that she and her sister Doris were on the stage at one time and were in the local pantomine at the old Barton Theatre. I know that Mum had a son before she was married and that when he was quite young he was sent to some kind of school, either a Reform School or a home for backward and difficult children and she never saw him again until he was twenty-one.

She and her sister Doris married two brothers and as they

both had seven children and all lived in Barton, there appeared to be a tremendous lot of Hardings, all very much alike and all causing much trouble to the police by their habit of using each other's names and identities.

Mum's family were the wildest and most notorious; Doris's children did tend more to working for their living and living with the people they had married, though they were often drawn into 'Harding rows' and often involved in shady deals with Mum's children.

I tell this history of Mum because I think it was her character which influenced her children. She was wild and unbalanced and undisciplined and no respecter of law and order. For some years after her marriage she used to appear in the chorus of the Barton Theatre Pantomime, even when she had five children. I have an idea that she was an amateur prostitute during the first World War, but she never admitted that. She did tell stories of the jobs she had taken during that war, one being a tram conductress, and she used to boast of the money she and others made by some method of trickery on that job.

From the stories her sons and daughters used to tell me, I should think they had a very disturbed and neglected childhood, though Mum herself always talked as if she had put her children first and struggled to feed and clothe and look after them.

For the various 'disasters' in her married life, she used to blame the 'old man', saying that he wouldn't work and was a drunkard. They were constantly being evicted and doing 'Moonlight flits' and always in debt. She often told one story of the old man leaving her and she got evicted for not paying rent, so she collected the six kids and walked them all through the snow to where he was living with another woman. She 'parked' the whole lot on the doorstep and made a terrible scene until he eventually found a home for them all and came back to her.

THE OLD MAN

The Old Man used to tell me stories occasionally and he blamed her, saying she was a wicked woman and completely mad and that she drove him to drink. He never said any of this in her presence, however; he was definitely frightened of her.

They have all told me stories of her terrible temper and how she had several times hit him with flat-irons, etc., and nearly killed him. She told me the same stories, but said it was because he used to go with other women and come home drunk.

I don't know much about the Old Man, except that he was supposed to have Jewish blood and was a tailor. He always said that his family were good class, that his sisters were musicians and 'singers of the opera' and that they had cast off him and his brother for marrying the wild B... sisters. His mother and father and sisters lived in Earl's Court in a big house, but they did not ever see them.

Mum was not particularly nice-looking, though she may have been attractive when young. She had 'style' and even then, when her children were grown up, she used to 'make up' and dress like her daughters, and she used to look very smart, though 'flashy'.

But the old man *was* attractive, not very tall, but well-built and dark, with dark brown hair, dark eyes and a ruddy, warm complexion.

All the children, except Jack, the eldest, who was not his, were like him and were very attractive, with a strong sexual attraction, both the boys and girls. They all attracted the opposite sex in a really remarkable way, which I think accounted for their marriages and love-affairs.

They all lived in a mad, cheerful, reckless way and were full of fun and vitality. They were John (known as John Harding), Dora, Elsie, Richard, Vincent, Marie and Ernest.

JOHN

John was six feet tall, strong and tough looking; he had been brought up in this home, somewhere in Wales, and had never learned to read or write, but had been trained as a butcher and a gardener and had won certificates for both, (so his mother said). There was a story connected with his escape from the home at the age of twenty-one. Mum said that she had never been allowed to see him and did not even know where he was. He knew that he had a mother somewhere in London and he

79

had escaped and come to London. It was only by chance he found his relations, and eventually his mother.

I don't know the details, but Mum said that 'they' tried to get him back again and they 'charged' her with concealing him. I've an idea she got convicted and served six months for this—at any rate she had been in prison at least once. But she said that eventually she and John won, and he remained free from then on.

There is obviously more to the story than this, but Mum never told a complete story, she never admitted anything that would be damaging to her kids. However, John seemed fairly sensible, though not intelligent, and while very tough and generally feared, had not, to my knowledge, been involved in any assaults on anyone—though Richard had.

Whenever John was mentioned in a family argument, one of them (not Mum) would say: 'Oh, John—well he's mad—he was brought up in an asylum, wasn't he?' But in my experience, his behaviour was, on the whole, less mad than some of the others. There is no doubt that the old man was afraid of John and so was Richard, so I rather think that Mum had used her strong eldest son to keep them in order; but that was before my time.

DORA

Dora was the first *Harding* child, about thirty when I first knew her. She had married young and had a son aged twelve; her husband was Jewish, a salesman, and she was living with him, but she had left him several times, and it was only because he loved her and always made desperate efforts to get her back that they were still together.

At that time she was having an affair with a middle-aged man with money; everyone in the family knew and helped her to meet him secretly, etc., but Jack, the husband, also knew, but pretended he didn't, because he did not want to lose her.

She had another child, a girl, aged four or five, who was assumed to be the child of this other man, though Dora strongly denied this when it was hinted by other members of the family. There were constant scenes and uproars between her and Jack, and her and the other man, usually at Mum's, in which all the members of the family who were present took part. On one occasion I remember Jack crying and begging her—literally on his knees—not to leave him, in the presence of several of the family and the kids and one or two 'outsiders', like me.

ELSIE

Elsie was the second child. She was twenty-six and also had been married very young and had a daughter aged about eight. She had left her husband and now lived with a Jew known as 'Maurice'. She was the only Harding who loved her partner more than he loved her and their frequent rows were because of his infidelity to her.

The reason I mention the fact that the old man was half-Jew and Jack and Maurice were Jews, is because during rows their various partners and the rest of the family frequently called them 'dirty Jews', etc., and blamed all their faults on the fact that they were Jews. One would have thought that the Hardings were anti-Jewish, but in fact they were not. Their arguments were always completely wild and illogical. They used also to call each other and the 'outside' women, such as me, 'dirty whores' and 'bloody prostitutes', during rows, though they had nothing against whores and had several friends who were recognised prostitutes. They also, I suspect, did a bit in that line themselves; at least I know Dora did during the recent war.

RICHARD

Richard was the third Harding and was twenty-four when I met him. He had married when he was nineteen and his wife had left him about a year after his marriage—or he had thrown her out—I was never quite sure. He had one son, aged four, who was in the care of the wife's mother most of the time, though there were occasions when the mother-in-law came and gave the child to Mrs. Harding saying she was not going to help him any longer because Richard would not pay towards his keep. As Richard very rarely worked and was often in prison, it was no use trying to force him to pay for the child. The kid was handed to and fro for some time until Richard started to live with a girl who offered to take the child because she was led to believe that nobody wanted him. But when she told the wife and her mother this, there was a tremendous uproar and she was told how much Violet (the wife) loved the child and that if she wanted a kid, she could have one of her own, she wasn't having hers. She, the wife, was living with another man, and by now had two other children. After that they never brought the child to the Hardings again and there were no more demands for money.

VINCENT

Vincent came next to Richard and was so like him that they were often taken for each other and many people thought they were twins. He was much quieter and more thoughtful than Richard and not so reckless and wild. He had been sent to Borstal for three years when in his 'teens and Mum said this accounted for his quietness. At the time I met him he was living with a girl called Iris Jones—she was always called her name in full by the Hardings—never Iris. Usually it was 'that Iris Jones', and I think this was because they did not approve of her and thought she was not good enough for Vincent; in a sense she wasn't—she was very coarse and ignorant and a dirty, lazy slut about the house.

She had a child when Vincent went to live with her, the child of a friend of the boys' who had refused to marry her. It was Mum's influence that prevented Vincent from marrying her, but as the time went on and she had two children by Vincent they more or less accepted her.

Vincent finally married her at the beginning of the recent war, when she was seven months pregnant with their third child. All the family turned up at the wedding at the Register Office, all dressed up to the 'nines'—only the bride being poorly dressed and looking ill and very obviously pregnant. Vincent was very kind to her always and faithful to her and thought the world of all the kids, including the bastard. In fact, Vincent was thought generally to be the best of the Hardings.

MARIE

Marie was the youngest girl and the prettiest. She spent almost every night in clubs and 'pubs' (in fact all the girls did) and was very much run after by men. She handled her men very cleverly—getting all she could out of them and giving them nothing, all this with Mum's advice and assistance. She had just started to live with a man called Bob, a tall, tough builder's foreman who had spent a good bit of money on her and promised her more. She was tired of being at home and having rows with Mum because she wouldn't do housework. She did not care at all for Bob (she didn't care for anyone but herself), she just wanted to be kept and have a good time.

ERNEST

Ernest was the youngest of the family (about seventeen) and was rather peculiar; he was subject to fits and was 'shaky'—that is, his hands were always shaking and he could not dress himself properly. He also spoke in a shaky, uncertain way, but he was not actually mentally deficient. He had never been to school and could not read or write.

Mum was very fond of him and very proud of everything he said and did that showed any sense at all. She never admitted that there was anything wrong with him, except the fits, and only spoke of that to 'intimates' of the family; he was six feet tall and well built. Whenever the other boys started one of their numerous businesses (usually in the motor trade), Mum insisted on them employing Ernest and paying him a wage. They said he was no good and wouldn't work and there were frequent rows about this. She also persuaded Bob to give him jobs in the building trade until Bob said he would get the sack himself if he kept employing Ernest on jobs.

DELINQUENCY

John had been in prison at least once and so had the old man. I think this was at the same time and was for some kind of partnership fraud. Maurice, the man with whom Elsie lived, had been in this too, but had only got three months; John and the old man had got twelve months each.

Vincent had been sent to Borstal with another boy (not a Harding) on a charge of attempting to steal a car. The family always said that they were only playing with the car and had not started it and that they knew the owner, but I don't suppose this was the whole story; I never knew what Mum herself had been in jail for. Richard had been in four or five times and was sentenced to three months again while he was living with the other girl. I think most of his sentences had been short ones and probably for motor offences. According to him, he had been concerned in smash-and-grab raids, but had only been employed by the gang as a driver of the car and had not done any actual stealing, nor had he shared in the spoils; he had merely been paid so much for the job. He was an expert and daring driver and knew all the 'back-doubles' in South London. He had also been in the stolen motor-car game and the stealing of loaded lorries. He used to boast that he had never been pinched for anything big, only small offences and had only received short sentences.

When I met him he had had his driving licence suspended for five years and had obtained a licence under an assumed name. Therefore, he was constantly taking a risk while driving—though he would not, under any circumstances, consider not driving.

Motors were his life and he was also a very good mechanic.

He could, and occasionally did, earn good money as a mechanic and he was not at all lazy, but he just could not stand the monotony of a regular job.

All the time I knew him he did not drink—he didn't like beer or spirits and seldom went into a 'pub'. In fact, none of the boys drank, though Mum and the girls did. I think Mum's insistence on the old man being a drunkard had frightened the boys off it and she certainly tried hard to keep John and Ernest from drinking, presumably because of John's mental instability and Ernest's tendency to fits.

Richard too had a very dangerous temper—he was noted for assaulting people, especially the police. When he did start drinking, some time later, it turned out that he became very good-tempered and merry when drunk and he never quarrelled with anyone when drunk, only when sober.

I believe this applied to the others also when they all started frequenting pubs.

84

Richard was incurably optimistic and never realised the risks he was taking. He never believed he would be caught and was absolutely enraged whenever he was caught. Indeed, he and the others had shown remarkable agility in getting out of trouble with the police and this was chiefly due to Mum's quick and clever brain. All the family always brought their troubles to Mum—whether criminal or matrimonial or anything else; she would always work out some scheme to help them out of trouble —from arranging an abortion for one of the girls to an alibi for one of the boys.

ATTITUDES

All the boys were hard workers at anything they wanted to do and were generous and good-natured (except in quarrels), and the girls were quick and good at housework and cooking when they had homes and were not living with Mum, and they kept their homes clean and bright and cooked good meals for their men and children, but they always managed to be dressed up and out every night.

If they had been brought up in a respectable household they would probably have been model citizens, but they had never known what it was to have peace in their home. In their childhood they apparently spent hours roaming the streets and had been dragged from home to home and lived in a constant turmoil of rows and fights between Mum and the Old Man.

They all regarded the police as their natural enemies and thought it perfectly right to 'twist' anyone, particularly landlords and furniture dealers and shop-keepers. They knew all the tricks for getting furniture and drapery and household goods (off tally-men) on the 'never-never' and then never paying for it. Richard boasted that all the others, except John and Ernest who were not married, had got their homes for next-to-nothing.

Wherever Mum lived, the others used to live as near as possible, and as Mum usually took a house which was made into several flats, there was always at least one married daughter and son living with her. Those who did not live with her visited Mum's frequently, so that the house was always full of people and kids and almost every day there was at least one row.

85

When a husband and wife quarrelled, they used to fight and throw things, so that one always had to be prepared to 'duck' as ornaments, pots of jam, even platefuls of dinner flew through the air. When a husband of a Harding's girl struck her, her brothers always came to her rescue and had a fight with him, but when a Harding's boy struck his wife, nobody would interfere. I have known Elsie to waken Richard up in the middle of the night and go and give Maurice a bashing, because he had hit her. But when Richard hit his girl, or Vincent his Iris Jones, or John bashed his girl, nobody took any part in the row, except a verbal one.

Once Richard and his girl had a row, ending in a fight (they were living in Mum's front room at the time) in the middle of the night, during which they threw things; Richard shouted and the girl cried and screamed and Richard finally knocked her out completely, after blacking her eyes and breaking a tooth, and though several of the family were in bed upstairs, only John, in the height of the uproar, came to the head of the stairs and shouted : 'For Christ's sake, Richard, get it over and let's get some sleep'. Although the Hardings fought amongst themselves and twisted one another and kept up all kinds of feuds and jealousies, they presented a united front against all outsiders, from 'the law' down to the various husbands, wives and lovers of the boys and girls. They helped each other to deceive their various partners although they didn't actually approve of such 'goings-on'.

MORALITY

They had a certain code of behaviour and morals and, more or less, they kept to it. They believed in keeping their homes clean and their husbands and children well-fed, though apart from that they made no attempt to train their kids morally. The kids were usually present at the terrific rows and knew all about their parents' 'affairs' with outsiders. They also believed in fidelity and were not promiscuous. That is, they did not have many lovers and usually stuck to the one they were with at the time. When they separated or were unfaithful, it was because of some other reason, not just sexual promiscuity.

86

The girls' idea was not to be unfaithful to their men but to go out every night and have a good time at any man's expense and give nothing except their company in return. Dora, of course, had a long-standing affair with a lover, but the excuse was that Jack, her husband, had been unfaithful to her and was not a good provider and she only had the one lover until the recent war when she took to a bit of part-time prostitution. This was done only for money and I have an idea that Jack knew about it, but kept his eyes shut.

They did not think it was wrong to break the law or make money dishonestly; they had never been brought up to think so and were not bringing their children up to think so either. In fact most of the family jokes were about how they had tricked the police or pulled off 'deals', and when all the family were gathered together they would relate such stories and roar with laughter.

None of them had any outside interests—such as sport, gambling or hobbies. They never read books or a newspaper and knew nothing about politics or world affairs. They didn't vote, except Mum.

Although born and bred in London, they seldom went outside their own area, B . . ., and they were lost in the West End. When any of them had to go up West they used to ask me the way—and I was a provincial and had not lived long in London.

The girls were only interested in dress and the life of the 'pubs' and the affairs of the family. The boys, only in the motor racket, 'crime' and the family affairs.

They had no interest in games, either as performers or spectators—I don't think any of them had ever been to a horse-race or a football-match or entered for the 'pools'. They were all strong and healthy and probably if encouraged when young would have been good at sports.

When Richard was sixteen he had run away and joined the Army and remained in for twelve months; when his regiment was going abroad his mother went and disclosed his real age and got him out of the Army.

During this twelve months he had learned a lot about horses —apparently he had been in a cavalry regiment and he had liked this—had learned how to groom and attend to horses and was learning how to ride. He had loved the horses and apparently been happy. He had also had some boxing training in the Army and had shown much promise as a boxer.

He was a good 'sport' and could take punishment. It was only in his outside life that he was a bully and this was because Mum had always taught them all to hit first and argue afterwards. They were all rather stupid and slow in argument, so that they preferred to get their own way by physical strength. In spite of this tendency to fight (the girls also settled their differences with women and sometimes men by fighting), they were all very likeable and good company and were popular wherever they went.

When Richard was in the Army or staying in Manchester, when Vincent was in Borstal, or John in the 'home' or working in Oxford for a year or so, they were well-behaved, enjoyed learning anything and gave no trouble.

Whenever any of the boys were away outside the radius of Mum's and the 'caffs' and 'pubs', they did not 'get into trouble' in any way.

As they didn't gamble or drink, they had no desire for money, except to live in reasonable comfort and dress well. But the boys were all very easily influenced by people more clever than themselves, as they had been influenced and dominated by their mother, and it just depended whether the influence was bad or good. Mum did not actually incite them to crime but she wanted to keep them all dependent on her and under her domination and resented them keeping away from the home as they would do if they were working and living with a wife or lover, so that when they complained of a job, as anyone would do from time to time, she was always full of sympathy and usually suggested some 'scheme' for making money, in which she would be involved; not actually an out-and-out, like burglary, but some sort of 'racket' usually connected with the motor business and usually 'dodgy' in some way.

They were also used by the numerous motor-men of South London, garage proprietors, second-hand car dealers, haulage men, to do any 'dodgy' or dirty job that came along. Because they were tough, not afraid of the law and would tackle anything.

Although the Hardings were a notorious family in South London and very much known to the police, they were not 'bad' at all and given the right upbringing and influences would have been good workers, good sportsmen, and honest, simple and attractive people. They were not vicious, mean, hypocritical drunkards, gamblers, cruel, nor dirty in behaviour, manners or speech. They did, of course, use 'bad' language constantly, because they had limited vocabularies and simply did not recognise it as 'bad'. For instance 'f...' was a household word, used constantly by all of them, including the kids, but when I once used 'f...' in the correct sense, they were all genuinely shocked. Richard and the other boys used to frequently call people a 'c...', but when I, in one of my more outspoken moments called a c...a c..., Mum told me she wouldn't have such talk in her house. In fact 'sex' never was discussed in the house and I never heard any of them tell dirty stories.

THIRD GENERATION

As far as I know the younger generation have not shown any signs of following the family way of life. They are doing fairly well at school, are not problem children, and are more interested in reading, games, and the cinema than their parents ever were. The two who have reached working-age (who have grown up during the last war), have both got good jobs and stuck to them, so far at any rate.

★   ★   ★

We have seen into some homes and into individual minds. What, then, of the fuller *consequences* of the delinquent process? Mass-Observation has collected a great deal of material from the organisations set up to cope with the effects of the phenomena we have been describing. For present purposes a small selection of such documents will illustrate the general pattern, and it is now time to examine a few.

IX

APPROVED?

L IFE at Borstal— the focal end of all delinquency—is very strictly codified in regard to punishments by Statutory Rules and Orders. In fact, about one-tenth of *Borstal Regulations, 1936* (the latest version), are explicitly concerned with offences against discipline, and restraints. Some of the paragraphs dealing with corporal punishment read as follows:

59. (1) If any inmate convicted of felony is charged with :—
    (*a*) Mutiny or incitement to mutiny,
    (*b*) Gross personal violence to any officer or servant of the institution,
the Governor shall, forthwith, report the name to the Visiting Committee, and the Chairman shall thereupon specially summon and cause as many as possible and in any case not less than three members of such Committee, two of them being Justices of the Peace, to assemble and enquire into the charges on oath in the manner provided by Section 5 of the Prison Act, 1898 (*a*); and such members may determine concerning the matter and make awards under their powers as set forth in Regulation 58, or, in the case of a male inmate convicted of felony, order corporal punishment, in addition to or in lieu of any such awards.

(2) Whenever an order for corporal punishment is made, ... such order shall not be carried into effect until it has been confirmed by the Secretary of State.

(3) The order for corporal punishment shall be duly entered in the prescribed manner, ...

61. Confinement to a room, corporal punishment, or restric-

tion of diet shall in no case be awarded unless the Medical Officer has certified that the inmate is in a fit condition of health to sustain it.

63.   (1) All corporal punishments within the institution shall be attended by the Governor and the Medical Officer.

(2) The Medical Officer shall inmediately before the punishment is inflicted examine the inmate and satisfy himself that he is in a fit condition of health to undergo the punishment.

. . . . .

(4) The Governor shall enter in the corporal punishment book the hour at which the punishment was inflicted, the number of lashes or strokes inflicted, and any orders which he may have given as to remission.

. . . . .

(6) The number of lashes or strokes inflicted on an inmate of eighteen years of age or over shall not exceed thirty-six, or an inmate under eighteen years of age, eighteen.

Arbitrary corporal punishment, 'bashings' or blows struck in anger are not even *alleged* in any of our Borstal material, subjective or imaginative, though some of it is sometimes self-pitying. The physical threats in Borstal life include solitary confinement; de-grading; deprivation of association, of gratuity, earnings, or of the right to play games; postponement of letters and visits; two grades of restricted diet; and 'deprivation of mattress'. But they exclude any sudden and unforeseeable violence from prison officers.

There is some suggestion, oddly enough, that this is not always the case in Approved Schools. Oddly, because Approved Schools might be expected to be less tough than the Borstals to which their more refractory inmates are sent.

In the following self-told case history of a Borstal boy the difference between the boy's *attitude* towards Remand Home, Probation Officer, Approved School and Borstal is the most striking feature. It is not suggested that all this lad says is *true* in the factual sense of being an entirely objective report of events. But it bears the mark of *subjective* truth, and the con-

91

clusion—rather six years' Borstal than go through Approved School treatment again—certainly reflects a deeply felt subjective reality.

Whatever the facts were, this boy was very likely exceptional and quite exceptionally unfortunate in his experiences. In common with all the documents presented in this report, the story must not be read as 'typical', nor yet as necessarily a-typical. It is just one boy's own version of his personal career of crime and treatment to date.

Here is the boy's own text (to be read of course with reservations)—

1. A BOY COMES TO BORSTAL

On the morning of the 9th I woke early and lay in bed thinking and wondering, for that day I was going to be transferred from the Remand Home to an Approved School in ... shire. At 6.30 an officer came into the dormitory and shouted, 'Come, on, get out of those beds, or else there is a bucket of water waiting to be emptied.' I was one of the first out of bed, and having made up my bed I went for a wash, and having done this, I sat on my bed and continued to think about my journey. I was deep in thought when all of a sudden there came such a blow across my face that it nearly knocked me off the bed, and turning round I saw an officer standing there. He said, 'I have told you before not to sit on your bed. Get off it.' So, with a stinging ear and sore thoughts, I fell into line with the other boys, and we made our way to the dining hall.

As soon as I was ready we left the Remand Home, and soon arrived at ... station, where we walked up a long flight of steps and came out into the street. As we passed a sweet shop my guard said, 'Would you like some sweets?', and I quickly said, 'Yes'. So he gave me twopence and told me to ask for fruit drops, which I did. On coming out of the shop I could see nothing of my guard, and about two minutes later I saw him down the road, but not knowing London at all I had no idea of trying to escape as I was only fourteen and a half years old. I walked down the road to him and gave him the sweets which he told me to put in my pocket, which I did. We walked down the road a little further and were soon at the Main Line Station, where we went on to the platform to wait for the train that would take us to B...

We boarded the train and found an empty compartment and put what things we had in the luggage rack, and then stood at the window to watch the people on the platform moving about and boarding our train. It was all very exciting but I could not help thinking of my arrival at the school. The journey was pleasant and I was interested in the scenery. At about 11 o'clock my escort asked me if I would like something to eat, and I said 'Yes, please.' With this he pulled down a small case he had with him and started to give me pies, tomatoes and apples. I ate a pie and an apple and gave him the rest back. He ate two or three pies and then started to read a paper, and I got a book to read. I was soon disturbed by my escort, who was being sick all over the floor. When he had finished, he took hold of his belongings and we shifted to another compartment. The rest of the journey was smooth with no more stops, and at last we were at B... station.

The school is situated at the bottom of a hill, and when we had seen the bus out of sight we started to walk down a little pathway to the school. As we went down this lane affair we saw two boys leading a horse and cart. They were dressed in short trousers, leather leggings, jackets two sizes too big, and a cape round their shoulders. They did look funny. We walked round and came in sight of the building itself, and went to a door marked 'Official' and knocked. A man about thirty years old answered the door and told us to come in. We did this, and were shown into the Governor's room. He asked us if we had had a nice journey and what was the weather like when we left London. After I had been talking with him for about half an hour he went out of the room and called a boy in and told him to take me to the matron and get my clothes changed. When I had changed my clothes and had had a wash the boy took me up a flight of steps into a school room and told one of the teachers that I was a new boy. The teacher told me to sit at the back and brought me some books down and told me to copy something off the blackboard.

93

I had been writing for about five minutes when I heard the teacher call a boy's name. The boy came out and received a bashing for some sums which he had done wrong in the morning. The teacher hit him on both sides of the face, and then punched him in the stomach and finally kicked him in the backside and sent him back to his seat. When he got to his seat he was still crying, and the teacher went to him and told him to pipe down and gave him another smack across the ear. After seeing this, I felt a bit rotten and homesick.

We had tea and then played cards, and at last I was shown to my bed. I slept sound that night, for I was tired, and woke up refreshed. I had a cold strip wash and dried myself on a damp towel and then did half an hour's work and then had breakfast. At about half-past four in the afternoon I asked the teacher if I could go to the lavatory and he said 'Yes'; so I left the schoolroom and, instead of going to the lavatory, I ran across some fields to the main road, and by the time I reached it it was quite dark... I walked about a mile and then got a lift in a car to B... I was wandering about B... when a car drew up beside me and two officers got out and took me in the car and started on the way back to the school. When I got back, I had some supper in the Officers' Mess and then went to bed. They did not punish me for absconding, as I was a new lad.

The time after this seemed to go quick and Christmas was on us before I knew where I was. I went home for Christmas for two weeks, and then had to settle down again. I can remember one morning up in the school room when a boy spilt some ink on his book. The teacher got hold of him and punched him on the nose so that the blood started to pour all over the place. He then gave him eight strokes with the cane and we could see the marks on his backside for weeks afterwards. One Sunday morning we went for a walk in the country and one boy with us named S... messed his trousers, and, when he got back, the officer took his trousers off and rubbed them all over his face. The stuff went into his eyes, his mouth, and his hair, so that you could not see his face from the brown mess.

I worked in the school room for nine months and then went into the carpenter's shop where I did not get on very well. One

94

day the Governor came up to me and said, 'How would you like to go home tomorrow?' I said, I should like to very much, and he told me to wait outside the stores in the morning at 9 o'clock. This I did, and when I had received a case containing clothes I got changed. At one o'clock we started in his car for London and arrived there at 8.30. I managed to catch a train for R... and arrived home at 11.15. I had only been home a day, however, when I received a letter saying that if I did not get a job within four days an officer would come down and fetch me back for another year and seven months. On the next morning I got a job as errand boy for a greengrocer. I could not find a decent job, however, and started to go wrong again. I first started by stealing from my boss to make more of my wages which I earned. But I got the sack because someone told my boss that I had been to an Approved School. I had a hard time getting work and all the time I was unemployed I was getting worse and worse. I had to get a living somehow, and I could not get it by honest means, so, I had to get it by other means, which is the same thing as saying by stealing. At last I was caught red-handed in a shop with a man of forty-two at 4 o'clock in the morning. I was tried and sent to Wormwood Scrubs prison, and then was sent back to the Approved School.

When I arrived I received a sound bashing up from the Head and from the officers, and in two days I was properly fed up, and within a week I ran away again. This time it was at 5.15 in the morning... I walked and ran all the way from 14 miles outside B... into B... and then on to C..., and then D... and finally ended up at E... I was sleeping under a hedge when a policeman came up and asked me my name, and I replied, 'Bill Sykes'. He asked me where I lived and I said I had left home to look for work. He did not believe me and asked me to turn out my pockets, and he found a letter with the address of the School on it. He took me to his cottage and his wife gave me some tea and bread and cheese and cakes. I had not eaten since 5 o'clock the previous day and I was half starved. When I had finished, the policeman telephoned to the station and a car came and fetched me to the station. When I got there the Copper third degreed me and tried to make me tell them that I

95

had stolen something. I slept in a cell that night, and in the morning a car came and fetched me back to the Approved School.

When I got back there the Head gave me a hot time with his cane which he kept in pickle and my backside hurt me so much that I could hardly sit down. I also received the same the next day. I once more ran away.

This time I hid in a haystack all night and could not leave because it was surrounded by officers. Anyhow on the next night I managed to steal one of the officers' car and get away in it... I got as far as C... when the petrol ran out. So I had to leave the car and go on foot and it was not long before I got caught by a Speed Cop who took me back to the school.

The next night I went into the Governor's office. First he started by getting hold of me by the hair and giving me two black eyes. He then kicked me in the stomach and winded me. I ran to the fireplace and picked up a poker and threatened to hit him with it. Then two officers pounced on me and held me down whilst the Head beat me something terrible. When I got to my feet it was only to be knocked down by a terrific blow on the mouth. He then laid me across a chair and gave me fourteen strokes with the cane on the back and backside. After this he took off his coat and belted me all round the office. I must have lost consciousness because I remember coming round crying, 'Father, father, stop, stop.' I was completely out of my head. When he had finished beating me he led me down to the showers, kicking me all the way. I had a cold shower which brought me to my senses a bit. When I was putting on my shirt again I saw that it was covered with blood. When I had dressed, one of the officers went to fetch the best boxer in the school. When he arrived, we went into the gym and the boy put on boxing gloves and I was made to fit on a pair, and then the boy was told to tan me. But as he was one of my mates he refused, only to be told that if he did not do so, he would get a beating. So we started, but he never hit me and I could not hit him as I was nearly all in.

My face, when I woke in the morning, was a sight. I could hardly see, for my eyes were nearly closed up and my mouth was swollen about an inch out, and it was all cut and hurt me to eat . . . one ear had been bleeding in the night, for there was blood all over the pillow . . . I was put in a field to work next morning and I was that all in that I fainted for the first time in my life.

Well, things went on all right for a week and at the end of two weeks my face had healed up and I escaped once again and got all the way down to my home in Sussex, about 270 miles from the school. I was again caught and handed over to the police. I was sent to Wormwood Scrubbs Prison when I received three years Borstal for a shop-breaking offence. *And I can only tell you that I would rather do six years Borstal than go through all treatment again what I had at the Approved School.*

★   ★   ★

Strange and improbable as such accounts may seem, this one is not unique in our files. Senior prison officials have themselves spoken to us with concern of the present system of Approved Schools, which is perhaps as antiquated and incoherent as that of *Old People's Institutions* recently revealed in the Nuffield Report (*Old People*) by a committee under the chairmanship of Mr. Seebohm Rowntree.

Moreover, the Press and the courts have lately paraded the extraordinary things that can happen with the case of the six boys in a northern Approved School who shot a master—and intended to murder the Head. That school is probably an admirable one. But of others we hear fearful things.

When we arrive at the next step in a delinquent's 'career' things are clearer, more cut and dried.

X

HIGHBROW DELINQUENT

'THE Medical Officer shall report to the Commissioners through the Governor any case of an inmate whose mental health appears likely to become impaired by continued discipline or treatment.'

(Borstal Regulations, Para. III.)

'Psychology is highly specialised, and is very, very technical. I don't know much about it. As a layman I can say that there is nothing psychologically wrong with many of the boys who pass through our hands.'

(Borstal Official in conversation with M.-O.)

'Oh, the misery that's caused by selfish or unimaginative mothers!'

(MONICA DICKENS, 'Women are So *Cruel*', *Women's Own*, 17th January 1947.)

'Love is impossible if hate is entrenched. In the human mind, unlike the dog's, such a mood of hatred tends to perpetuate itself through phantasy... The child thus comes to be haunted by bad objects, with the familiar result that he comes to regard himself as a bad object.'

(JOHN BOWLBY, *Forty-four Juvenile Thieves*.)

We can best penetrate Borstal through the subjective stresses of a boy who dramatises his mental journey thus :

We were locked in the basement room. Father had been irritable that night and told 'Gin-soak' not to 'stand any nonsense'. Then he burst out of the house, accompanied by a series of

98

violent noises and calling all the time for Mother. She came in, and wet us pretty thoroughly with some highly maternal kisses then rushed to her husband's side. I think they went to a dance hall.

Harold, who was two years older than I, and a good deal more powerful, although only seven years old, jumped from his bed and instructed me to act as his accomplice. The plan was elaborate for his undeveloped brain—a raid on Mother's room. We were to carry off any edibles or toys we found.

I always distinctly remember, that night, in that room—the sickly unwholesome odour of cheap scent, underwear and finery strewn about in confusion. And always has it left its impression on me. I vowed from thenceforward never to consort with a member of the female sex. After that night I had a loathing for my Mother's cheap sentiment. A stumbling-block was my position, I knew that I was a check to their enjoyment. My existence which followed was a life of extremes. Dad would have a car one month and the next we would all be instructed in the ways of severest economy.

Several emotions conflicted in the years following. Shame at school, because of shabby clothes, and because I could not become a participant in the games. Neighbours withdrawing themselves and their children from our family. They overheard the violent quarrels between my parents. They were quarrelling—then a reconciliation, more quarrels.

My brother was always admired and feared by me, he was very English—reticent. At the age of ten, there were two additions to the family, Pamela and two years later, John. Pamela was violently spoilt and petted, until it made her obstreperous, and then she was cursed for a further obstacle in my parents' way of amusement.

Father was only thirty years old, and after four years of hell in France, deserved enjoyment, but I suppose, failure to control his sexual desires was his real stumbling-block and obstacle. We were a family of individuals, an unconventional mob of emotional clashes. Father had to spend a couple of months in prison for debt! Harold, my brother, thieving steadily from a paper shop, where he had obtained a part-time situation. Pamela, almost killed in an accident! I was blamed and punished for not conducting her from school properly. Father worked steadily at driving jobs, always he was able to 'fiddle' (supplement his wages by systematic thieving from his employers). I admired my Father, he was a MAN. He was a really *good* man. He stole for his family, he had very few vanities, and remained faithful to his wife, although maternity was playing havoc with her physical attractions. All his quarrels were for the good of his family. Quarrels about bad cooking, false economy, wasting money on cheap finery; children looking pale and uncared for. Of course we were always involved, always we heard those same curses. 'Whore!' Always that same filthy repartee, 'I earned my living on my back before I *met you*!'

In later years I often wondered how much of these inane curses and bravado were true. I never admired my Mother, she was very pathetic. A woman with wonderful maternal instincts and emotions, capable of deep love but never fully developed. She was a drag, no material use whatever to the family. At times she was deeply religious. Father cursed the Christian Church, 'a bloody, frail organisation of the blind, the lame, the satisfied, the conventionally genteel, the stupid and half witted. Bastards! full to the brim of cant and timid orthodoxy.'

He was a fine man, warped by the war, and the frustration of his wordly plans. The war had made him crude, and his crudities made me sensitive and shy. I longed to escape to some haven of peace, love, and tranquillity. It was he who brutally but totally unconsciously first made me realise the deep emotions as yet unrevealed. I was in bed, trying to read a mystifying book called, 'Sex in Youth' which I had found somewhere. I could not understand what the book meant, until Father came into my room, saw me with the book and thrashed me! My brother then explained, in Father's own crude style, the mysteries of sex. All this time I had been very depressed, by the jeers of my fellow schoolmates, and the occupation to which I was tied, nursemaid to my younger brother and sister. I resented this and complained regularly to my harassed parents. Harold had by this time half won a scholarship, which entitled him to go to a Central

School. Harold, however, was built more on my father's lines, and asked if he could not go to sea instead. Arrangements were made, and while a whole year passed by, nothing developed. I then sat for the scholarship and managed to pass easily. It was then that I saw my life in front of me. Education! It would enable me to gain a position in this world, where I would be able to be eccentric without loud disapproval. I was very happy and gaily picked ... College as my new school. ... College, however, refused to have me, I truly think this was on account of my social status, and not because of failure in their niggardly little entrance examination. Father said he couldn't pay anyway, so I chose another school to apply—I passed their exam.

Then the blow fell! No money! How could he keep me there? Why! They only give him an allowance of four pounds a year!

I cursed my Father, the British system of Education, and my maker; and depressed violently, I soon discovered how I could *hate*! I envied bitterly the smart youths who wore college caps, and pretended indifference by coarse jibes.

I decided to accompany Harold to the Training Ship. As brothers we were queerly matched. He was sturdy, complacent and steady. I was passionate, emotional and very weak. Although I liked him and admired him tremendously, I think he despised me for a weakling. On my decision he was very annoyed, he wanted to start on his own, to free himself entirely from this mad screaming family. Finally, we went. Harold settled down and won the admiration of the majority of the boys on the ship. I was humiliated, never had I mixed with so many boys. I hated them, hated their coarseness. I wanted something different. I had had coarseness and crudities for so long, could I not have a change? I felt terrible, always crying, cursing, always being jeered at. I blindly and passionately cursed my silly sentimental mother for endowing me with such unmanly qualities, such a sensitive nature. I slowly became more coarse, more crude, trying to take my place as an ordinary member of the company. But always I shuddered inwardly, always I dreamt, and cried for some beautiful pure angel to carry me out of such sloth. I learnt to masturbate and tried to drug myself. I imagined

101

I could forget my silly sensitivity. I thought I was reaching that stage when everything changes, and turns out all right. But more and more I hated my own crude passions, and both seemed to develop. My brother saved me from many humiliating scenes, and I was glad he could prevent me becoming the victim or the accomplice in some vile act, such as sodomy.

When my brother was sixteen and I fourteen, we both left. He left because he was old enough to go to sea, as he went. I left, because my parents refused to pay the small weekly payment necessary for my upkeep.

The captain got me a job in an old country house as a pantry boy.

This termination of my sea career was an added bitterness. I had studied navigation, trigonometry, logarithms and algebra. I cursed those wasted hours, cursed my parents, my maker, but most of all I cursed Society in general, for their scurvy treatment of my parents and I.

An incident to illustrate the further filth and coarseness I had to mix with at this first job.

A young girl of about seventeen years with the charm and the manner of a country wench. After the usual intimacy in which we worked, and talked, she approached me one night after supper.

'Cecil, do be a dear and give me a hand with that new bicycle I've bought, the tyre's punctured.'

'Sure.' I liked Joan, despite her rather crude jokes, which she constantly repeated.

We made our way to the garage, and I quickly repaired the tube, damaging my hand very slightly in the process.

'I'll put a bit of bandage on it ... come to my room.'

I followed her into her small bedroom, and I was lost, despite the childish resolve that I had made in my Mother's room long ago.

All my disappointments, all the frustrated plans, my weak character, and my contact with the baser side of youth's nature, made me try and forget myself in an orgy of sexual abandonment. I failed, still that sensitive streak in my character forced its way to the top.

How I longed for someone to love, a pure love! I wanted to be able to appreciate beauty, but I was not educated to it. My bestial environment, my nature made up of queer streaks from heredity. A streak of animal passion, of coarseness, overwhelmed my gentler side. I could have fought against it perhaps successfully, but for the savage, relentless bad luck which had followed me in my opportunities.

Father wrote to me kindly, giving an account of a job which was open, 'a damn good job' he called it.

I went home, I thought after my absence of nearly three years I might be able to see things more clearly.

No good job!

Bitter disillusionment! Bitter disappointment!

I cursed my parents and found a job making wireless cabinets. When I had reached the age of fifteen, I secured a slightly better situation in a laundry.

I left home, I couldn't stand it, I used to grow hysterical and swear at my mother like a madman.

Not a single friend had I made. I bought an old motor cycle and loved it! Really loved it! It was the nearest I had ever been to real happiness.

I changed my job again, and found I had made a mistake, I had to live on a pittance of eighteen shillings a week!

The landlady's daughter came to my room one evening, she was a blousy woman of about thirty, handsome in a large featured way.

Two weeks rent please was demanded of me. I burst out crying and poured into the sympathetic ears a false cheap sentimental story. She used to sleep with me after that. I read a lot of Deeping and other romantic and sentimental authors' books.

I cried to my God for help for a little will power to try and control the result of my tangled upbringing.

Then I broke down, stole my employer's money, and descended on London with twelve pounds and a spirit that cried for drugs. A week of drugged existence in the form of drink, cinemas, and Hyde Park prostitutes.

I gave myself up, with the hope in my mind that it would start me afresh.

It did, it started me afresh in the contact of beasts, foul stories, bestial natures, filthy debauchery and bitterness.

Twenty-five long dreary months of hopes, disappointments, rows, promises, hatred, depression, sexual repression, torture of mind and spirit. I stole incessantly and just as regularly got found out and punished.

I had through my Father a deep contempt for the Church. I was never baptised or christened, but I was confirmed on the Training Ship.

This was a farce; proving in my receptive mind that the Church was indeed an organ of timid convention, and caring only for the 'right' people. Unconventionalists and Individualists were not catered for by the Church of England.

I belonged to or joined an organisation at the prison. The Regional Surveyors, we used to visit cathedrals, abbeys and old buildings of historical interest. I was acquainted, through this body, with a number of clergy. We stayed a week-end at an old vicarage, at a small town or village. While here, I sacrilegiously looted holy wine, alms boxes and any other articles of any value to me. Also, while away on a week-end expedition, I foolishly allowed myself to be caught with another fellow, in a room with two girls. The outcome of this episode was disastrous, the Governor had the girls seen, had them sign a statement of negativity, and the friend and myself were held back from discharge for six months. On hearing this sentence my friend absconded, and was caught a week after and sent to R... The person who caused us to be caught and punished, by injudicious talking, also eventually came to R...

I hate to believe in black curses or any such superstition, but *every fellow* who stole that Holy wine, came back to another term of imprisonment.

Eventually I was discharged. The B.A. found me a job at a Motor Manufacturers. I secured some marvellous lodgings in West Kensington. It was a boarding house, run by an American woman and her very American daughter. My fellow lodgers were all working in offices. There were four girls and three of my sex. This was a semi-happy, half miserable time for me, with decent conversation, clean youths and girls, and a chance to secure that peace of mind. But no, I was envious of their position, of their clothes, of their relations and friends. I tricked the B.A. into giving me extra money, but I wanted a better paid job.

On my first night of freedom I was introduced to a young man, who had offered me his friendship. He was a son of a very old country family, with an Oxford Education, and Army and Colonies experience, and now held a job of some importance. I liked him at once, and when he used to invite me to dinners and cinemas I was wildly elated. He was a marvellously kind and understanding young man, but the friendship was doomed for failure. I, wishing to credit him, looked for some means of securing better clothes. I wanted to treat him to a dinner. I wanted to mix with his friends, but I knew it was impossible. After five weeks in London, I was still hating myself. Hating, for my scrounging at the B.A., hating for my continuous grumble for better pay. Hating myself, because I could not genuinely fall in love with one of my fellow boarders. These girls were extraordinarily sweet, and I believe, really pure.

I was sure now, sure that I could not love, had never been loved, bitterness overwhelmed me. I wanted love, longed to be understood. I was an Outcast; a young fellow—tragically young; with a gangrenous heart, a rotten, filthy, warped mind.

Then I went down—down. I left my nice boarding house, left my respectable job. I secured work in a hotel as a bartender. A very exclusive hotel, patronised by Americans, flat bloated capitalists. It was a job that brought me again in contact, in close association with people, whose finer natures had been obliterated by beast desires. I could have made a friend of one of those, and we could have helped each other perhaps to climb above these bestial natures. No one seemed to have the least desire to rise to the beautiful things of life, and my offers of a helping hand were rebuked.

It was then that I started thieving. An elaborate system of defrauding the post office. I was successful for many times. With the proceeds I stood my newly acquired friend a dinner, and bought some decent clothes. I started drinking a lot of spirits and drugged myself with false enjoyments. I had always wanted, all my life, to become a racing driver, so with my newly reaped riches I visited Brooklands frequently. I should like you to visualise my friends or those that wanted to be a friend. There was the fellow who had offered his friendship on my discharge. I had the happiest time of my life in his company. I met some of his friends, motored with him, dined with him. Always, however, the thought of my duplicity, my rottenness, spoilt these pleasures. I had the suspicion in my mind, the suspicion that nothing could eradicate, that he was a friend because he thought himself obliged to me, because of a hasty offer. It has always been the same, of all the people I have liked most, I have always felt that they were giving all and taking nothing.

My other friends were an ex-Borstal and his wife. He was very well educated and had a marvellous situation in a house-agents' office. He was awfully good to me, and I always confided in him. I had dinners with him and his wife many times, but I slowly started to drift away from him. He was good and had a good wife. I was a rogue, a material minded, coarse seeker after cheap thrills and false happiness.

I was regarded with a mixed amount of awe at the Hotel. The staff, seeing me in my fine clothes, of which I was immensely conceited, thought I was some gentlemanly pauper, who was forced by financial reasons to obtain such a low situation. I made no effort to check these thoughts, and revelled in my cheap glory. The girls working in the house were particularly amicable to me, and I had opportunities of intimacy which I invariably took.

So I lived, for another month. Keeping up appearances, lechery, thieving, drunkenness. On top of all, I still searched for the perfect love. That was the immense jest! I, the thieving scoundrel, looking for goodness and purity!

I was arrested.

Despair, black despair! attempts at suicide! Hope? communications from my friends. Resolutions. I could be out in six months, and then I would seek simplicity. I would have done too! By God's name I would!

Another three years! Cursed be that judge for a fool! My

fool mother, curse her! My unorthodox environments, those hereditary streaks in my character! Lack of guts! A fool, a poor fool! Searching, waiting for some love, some labour to which I might sacrifice myself.... Offers of friendship. No more! How my Maker must hate me! How I hate my Maker myself!

If I receive the encouraging news, that I shall be able to get out in nine months at the most, I shall not abuse it. I shall seek simplicity. If! I know I shall not! I know I shall escape! Cells, escape! Cells—Death? I hope so.

★   ★   ★

So much for the highbrow—or at least highspot—delinquent, his account itself a field day for the psychiatrist. A less coloured view is now due...

XI

INSTITUTIONS

'When we realise that the provocation to delinquency is con-
fused with its cause, that symptoms are mistaken for the disease,
we understand why there are so many false conceptions of what
should be done with the delinquent child and we wonder no
longer that treatment often fails. Without the discovery of the
deep underlying causes of delinquency, any cure is accidental.'

(AUGUST AICHBORN, *Wayward Youth*.)

'If you set up a sausage machine you need something to put
through it.'

(F. T. GILES, *The Juvenile Courts*.
Allen and Unwin. 1946.)

'I am firmly convinced that the present system of treating kid
crime with two pairs of velvet gloves is a mistake. There is
much more crime about than the official reports show. Much of
it is unreported to the police as folk are convinced that it is a
waste of time to take proceedings against children. Most of the
trouble comes from lack of parental control. State can't grumble
about this. Policy of the educationalists has consistently
taken kid control from parent into hands of teacher. Teachers
often women with airy-fairy notions about kids but not much
idea of the little devils out of class. Control by teacher is very
weak. I know what the staff think about the magistrates, etc.,
and it is not complimentary. I do know this. When the local
police kept a rod literally in pickle for local kids off the rails
there was less wilful damage to property, etc., than there is now.'

'The damned old women of both sexes who seem to get on to the benches are not logical.'

(Commercial traveller.)

'Girls in Borstal Institutions got a pleasant surprise yesterday when officials began calling them by their Christian names, instead of their surnames.'

(*Sunday Pictorial,* 19th January 1947.)

'The more the life of the institution conforms to an actual social community, the more certain is the rehabilitation of the child. There is a great danger in an institution that the individuality of the child does not develop along lines best suited to his needs but that rules are laid down in accordance with administrative requirements which reduce the child to a mere inmate with a number.'

(AUGUST AICHBORN, *Wayward Youth.*)

'I suggested at a Housemasters' meeting that all boys ought to be asked to write a diary on "Christmas at Borstal". The Governor put forward the opinion that it would be a very difficult thing to have done. "You see," he said, "many boys are incapable of writing anything, and if they wrote nothing, disciplinary action would have to be taken".'

(From a Borstal diary.)

Notes:

1. In Holloway Prison the privilege of using cosmetics was first conferred on the prisoners in August 1946. More recently the suggestion was officially considered that they might wear their own foundation garments.
2. Sex is not mentioned in Borstal Regulations.
3. Last year the N.S.P.C.C. investigated 41,720 cases involving 107,037 children; of these only 213 cases were dropped after investigation. Three-quarters of the cases concerned neglect, ill-treatment and assault, the vast majority of these, neglect.

It is difficult for any outsider to get inside institutions and prisons, and the elaborate arrangements which need to be made beforehand tend to preclude any observation of normal everyday activity there. On the other hand, officials who are in everyday contact with their institution and its inmates are precluded from telling of their experiences or systemising their observations in public by the regulations of the Service. Off-the-record conversations cannot be quoted, because even when heavily disguised and not assigned to individuals, such are the idiosyncracies and peculiar features of individual institutions that an impenetrable disguise would simply befog the issue. Thus if we say that a certain official having prepared a specialised memorandum in order to clear his mind on certain issues and principles involved in his job, was refused permission to show the memorandum privately to specialist colleagues outside the Service who could criticise it and offer suggestions, we are on safe but unilluminating ground. If we say more, and most certainly if we had seen the memorandum, or if we reported snatches of conversation from the Officer concerned, he would become recognisable, and perhaps be subjected to disciplinary action.

There is sense and nonsense in the situation. It means, however, that a great part of the information about life in institutes which is available to the general public comes either from very high officials, or from ex-inmates, or from a few bold spirits among the less exalted members who are more concerned with getting the facts known than with their own security and position.

The documents we present here are different in the sense that they do not come from people with the over-riding desire to publish—which, in the case of institutions, almost inevitably means to defend, or to expose. The informants, who wrote in confidence and by request, present (as in all such documents) a subjective view, but their biases are probably less vigorous, and certainly different from, those whose observations are normally published.

1. 'HOME' TO APPROVED SCHOOL

Note: It is a legal possibility for a child to end up in gaol having committed no other offence than those of being born of parents considered inadequate by the state; and of expressing his disapproval of the substitutes provided by the state by attempting to escape from them.

I was taken away from my mother and father and put in the Cottages Homes, with my sister, who was at the age of nine months, and I had just turn three years old. I was put in the Cottage Homes by the town Guardians, because my parents could not afford to keep us. In the Cottages Homes, I started to go to school, we were taken to School by a man, who also repair our boots.

At the age of seven I played truant from School, with another cottage Homes boy. We spent the first night out in the woods, and all we had to eat was chestnut and wild berries. We were out for three nights when my pal got ill. Well he layed in the bushes, and was cover all over with spots and I looked on my own chest and found that I had quite a lot of red spots on me, I got frighten and thought that I would be as bad as my chum Tubbs.

So I went to find somebody that would help us, and left my chum under the bush. I thought I will give myself up to the police. I walked quite two or three miles to the nearest house. On the gate was marked P.C. Roberts, and of course I did not know what P.C. ment, I walked to the front door and I found I could not reach the door nob or bell. So I started to look around the house when I heared a voice from the top bedroom say, 'What the hell do you want you cheeky Devil?' I began to cry and he came down to me, I told him that I had ran away from the Cottage Homes, and that my chum was lying in the bushes ill.

So he got his coat and then asked me, where my pal was, so I led him the way and we had quite a job to find him because I forgot where I had left him. At last just before sun set we found him fast asleep. He carried my chum back to his house, and he telephone for a Doctor and ambulance and I found that me and my chum were taken to a hospital. My chum was put straight into bed, and I went straight into a Doctor's room. I saw the Doctor, he switched on me a kind of big head light and then he took off all my clothes and had a good look at me. Next thing was I found a nurse bathing me, the nurse got me a small shirt and put it on me, then she took me along the corridor and took me to the room were my chum was and put me to bed.

I did not see that nurse again until the following morning. She came in with some warm water to wash us with. I found out from one of the nurses, that we had chicken pox. Round about one o'clock on Tuesday the Headmaster came to see us from the Cottage Homes. His first words were 'You learnt your lessons now young fellows.' He brought us some grapes and told us to eat them before the sister came in. I felt very frighten when I saw him come in the door. But he was quite friendly with us. But at that time we were glad to see his back go through the door.

When we had been in bed about five weeks the doctor said we could get up and walk around. When we got out of bed, we found nearly all the nurses giving us sweets and cake. When we had been out of bed for a fortnight, the doctor said it would be quite all right for us to go back to the Cottage Homes, the same afternoon, and when we saw the matron, she said 'I will give it to you little devils if you run away again.' My chum and I always kept walking together after that. After we had been at the Cottage Home a week, we were given the job of chopping wood for the fires in the morning, and getting the coal in the evening. We also had to clean twenty five pairs of boots every night, for the boys to wear to school next day. One night we did not clean the boots, we left them dirty, and the matron called us in her sitting room and said, 'Why have you not clean the boots?' and then took down our trousers and hit our bottoms with a hair brush, and my bottom was a bit blue the next morning.

I felt like running away again, but I didn't. I change my mind at the last moment. When I was nine years of age, I run away from the Cottage Homes with another boy and a sister of his. His sister enjoyed the first night out with us, but when we started to steal she got very frighten. We were in a place and we went in a house to ask for some water, but the people were out and we found a key under the flower pot and so we got into the house.

My chum found a watch and a ring which we thought were not worth anythink, and we found five shillings which was for the baker. When we came to leave the house we found that we could not find Betty who was my chums sister, we search the house high and low and could not find her anywhere, and all of a sudden we hear foot steps outside the house.

We look outside the front bedroom window and we saw a man come in the gate with Betty so we run out the back when we were caught by a policeman and taken to the Police station. We were return to the Cottages Home but we were bound over for 12 months under the sum of five pounds.

A tall man use to come and see us once a fortnight. Well I started running away from school when I was sent. Just before I was ten years old I was sent to an Industrial School. The first week or so there I did not like it because the school was in the grounds, my school teacher used to make me go without my playtime and do sums.

One day I decided to run away from there and I did. I got quite a long way, then I was caught and taken back to the Industrial School, when I got back, the Headmaster, said follow me and of course I did not know what he was going to do.

He took me in the Gym and said take your nickers down and lay me over the horse. I would not do so. I tried to run out. So he lock me in the Gym and went and got Mr. B... and Mr. R... to hold me on the horse while the Headmaster gave me ten cuts with the cane across my bottom, and I shall never forget the day.

When I was fourteen they took me out of the school class and made me work on the land, planting cabbages and so on. Every year we went to camp and we enjoyed the fortnight that we had at camp.

Just before I was at the age of sixteen the headmaster Mr. B... came up to me one evening and said, 'Well, son you will soon be leaving us, we have found you a job on a farm in Sussex.' On the morning I left I was sorry to leave my friends behind. I was given a piece of paper with the address on where

113

I was going to work and the headmaster gave me half a crown and took me down to the station in his car, and saw me off.

When I got to the farm where I was going to work I was met by a young man who was to be my boss. He asked me if I knew any think about farm work and I said 'No'. So he said you will soon learn. He give me my five shilling a week pocket money, and I did not have much time off to spend that I only had every other evening off.

My job was to get up at four in the morning and feed the cows and then go about two mile up the road to get the cows. When I had done that I had to give him a call by knocking on his door. I had only been working for about three months when one Friday morning he said to me hears your wages and give me a half a crown, and I looked at him and said, what about the other half a crown please Sir, and he turn round with a sly look and hit me straight in the face and knock me out.

He left me on the ground and all of a sudden his wife said to me whats come over you and I told her what had happen, and she went and told her husband off about it and told me to go to bed. Well I felt sick as anythink and his wife went and fetched the Doctor.

The Doctor said I would have to go to hospital and I was taken downstairs and put in the doctors car with to or three blankets around me.

I was taken to Hospital and the second day I was in a policeman come in and asked me all about my boss, and what had happen. So I told him the story right through, and there was another man by me on the other side of my bed putting everythink I said down in a note book.

Three days later my bosses wife came in to see me and started to cry, she told me that my boss has got three months in prison and showed me it in the newspaper. I felt very sorry for him. When I went back to the farm, I found my bosses brother in charge of it. I was surprise and he was very good to me, and my bosses wife told me to walk around for a day or two before I started work.

When my boss come out of prison, he began to hit me about again, so I told his wife and she try to help the best she could,

114

but it made no difference, he would not give any pay. So I told him I was going to leave, he said all right you got me in prison, so you got to stop here. One night I got out of bed and it was about two o'clock by my watch. I creep down stairs and walked ten miles to the station, and I went to Seatown.

When I got to Seatown I stayed at the Church Army Lodge for seven shillings a week. One evening about two months afterwards as I was walking round the golf links as a caddie I hear a voice shout out Billy and there sat near the ninth tee was my old bosses wife and she said, I would like to see you when you have been round. When I got into the caddie house I saw her look at me with a smile, and she said, how do you get along now, so I told her that I was a caddie and stayed at the church army for seven shillings a week and of course she sat in the shelter and I asked her if she was on holiday and she said no I am sorry to say I have left Mr. Walker because I do not like him, she told me that she was not married to him and how she came to live with him.

She took me round to her flat which was one room and to my surprice when we got in the house she kiss me and said, I am very fond of you Billy and when ever you are in danger of any kind let me know and I will help you and I kept going round to were she living and playing cards with her every evening.

About a month after I was picked up by the police for stealing a bicycle. When I went to court I was sentence to three years Borstal, and while I was in the cell at the back of the court Miss B...[1] came in to see me, and said I feel very sorry for you, Billy, but face it like a brave boy and look after yourself in Borstal and you will soon be out.

She asked me to write to her and said, what ever you do dont run away from Borstal. She said we may be parted but let us keep friends and come and see me when you come out of Borstal, and I said I would come to see her, when I got out of Borsstal. Well I will be able to tell her that I did not run away from Borstal.

---

[1] The Probation Officer.

2. BOYS' PRISON

Note: This impression is written by a youth who spent a period in the prison described, not for a criminal offence, but for a special reason.

The whole atmosphere and environment in a Boys' Prison suggest to the inmate at all times that he's a social outcast, not fit to mix with the outside world. He is shut away amongst other similar delinquents for a period of a few months with a continual infliction of hardship and no mention or suggestion of reform.

Sixteen, seventeen, eighteen, nineteen, twenty and twenty-one year old boys wasting months—precious months in prison, languishing in cells, sewing mail bags, cleaning, scrubbing or digging ditches. Not only is it a negative form of existence in-asmuch as it's a waste of valuable time, with no attempt at reform, treatment, or even an opportunity to gain satisfaction from some form of constructive life. It is even worse because all this time the boy is thinking of himself and talking to others, swapping experiences, telling exciting yarns of conflicts with the police and teaching each other fresh and original methods of leading a life of crime. They resolve also (this particular type) to 'Get even', 'Make sure the cops don't catch 'em next time', etc. etc. They are almost unconsciously and almost always inevitably falling deeper and deeper not so much into the pit of crime and delinquency as into the even more deplorable pit of frustration and repression which in its turn leads either to delinquency or neurosis.

Half of the warders swear and make fun of the weak boys and of all those who give an opportunity, and all of the warders bully everybody.—Is this the sort of behaviour the only supposedly law-abiding persons present should adopt?

There were about 10 homo-sexuals in this prison when I was there—all grossly perverted in their psychological make-up. The warders make fun of them when they get the chance, and when in small groups (e.g. when bathing), they are encouraged to tell their experiences and are greeted with laughs and 'Go on—yes —tell us more', by warders as well as boys. These homo-sexuals

116

cling together to preserve their abnormality, when in the exercise yard they often walk about arm in arm, giggling to each other and using the various gestures and mannerisms of their kind.

No attempt, or at least no serious attempt, is made to stop them or their 'teasers'. Punishment is obviously so futile in this case, it merely ensures them continuing their life of a male prostitute on release and being more careful so as to avoid a further conviction; treatment by a qualified medical psychologist is the only safe course to take.

Many persons convicted on a 'suspect' charge admitted previous misdemeanours but vigorously protested against their latest conviction—I had every reason to believe their stories, they were continually protesting that they had no wrong or delinquent intentions when they were 'picked-up'. They were very bitter against the police and all authority that had contributed to send them to prison.

They said that everybody was against them : 'What chance do you stand when you've been in here once? They can always "pick you up" again on suspicion and then back you come here again.'

I noticed several cases of over 21's who had managed to convince the authorities they were only 20. As Wormwood Scrubs was the alternative to the Boys' Prison they naturally preferred to avoid that place if it was at all possible.

There was one person in particular who was a most undesirable character to mix with the boys. He was twenty-one and an army deserter. He was for ever explaining to all who would listen, the fairness and the worth of stealing £600, hiding it, and receiving a nine months' sentence (three remissions). He himself had done this and was very pleased with himself and said he thought it was well worth it, he had £600 to go out to.

3. Y.P. INCIDENT

(From a report by a woman prison officer, 1946.)

There are altogether eight different work parties, as well as other odd jobs to which prisoners can be allocated. The kitchen work is done mainly by Brownies, or Young Prisoners under twenty-one. Not all prisoners under twenty-one are graded Y.P.s; the decisions rests with the Deputy Governor.

The grading Y.P. carries many privileges. Y.P.s may receive and write letters every fortnight for the first three months, and after that, if their behaviour merits it, once a week. They may have visits once a fortnight instead of once a month, as is the rule for other prisoners. There are many more unofficial privileges—punishments are lighter, and the staff are comparatively more lenient.

The kitchen workers are unlocked earlier than the others, and taken over to the kitchen to start working on the breakfasts at 6.30 a.m. They are the last back for dinner, usually being returned to their cells by the Kitchen Officer between 1 o'clock and 1.30 p.m. They return at 2 o'clock to their work, and are locked in for the night at 6 p.m.

Another job reserved for Y.P.s is gardening. Gardening parties are taken out by a gardening instructor officer. These instructor officers get anything from 5/- to £1 week more than ordinary officers, only when engaged in instruction. The gardening party usually combines coaling as part of their job, filling the scuttles and buckets for all offices and mess rooms.

The kitchen officers are always much more irritable than any other officers, probably because their hours are much longer. They start at 6 a.m. and work till 6 p.m. one day and from 6 a.m. to 2 p.m. the next. In addition to their long hours the kitchen workers are invariably Brownies, and much more spirited than the older prisoners. They cannot be punished as severely for minor offences as older prisoners, and their officer consequently is obliged to nag and shout at them all day long.

The prisoners are naturally secretive, and to the casual observer they appear to be quiet and orderly. Occasionally a prisoner has a 'smashing up' fit, probably caused by the strain of having to endure eighteen hours' solitary confinement out of the twenty-four. In such a case the prisoner will smash up every article of furniture in the cell, tear her blankets and clothes to shreds, and then beat on the door and scream.

On one occasion during lunch time there was trouble with four Y.P.s. These girls had managed to shut themselves into one cell, having first locked the doors of the three empty cells to allay suspicion; and were not discovered until after lunch, when the officers came to unlock. They had barricaded the door of the cell in which they were so that it could not be unlocked. As soon as they were discovered, all the other prisoners in every part of the prison were locked in again, and fifteen officers, with the aid of two members of the engineering staff, were detailed to get them down into the punishment cells in the underground part of D Wing, known as D-1s. After all else had failed the engineers turned hoses on them through the hole in the wall, which had been stuffed up with bedding; then the lock was taken from the door, and after much heaving and pushing it was opened. A belabouring of heads, and punching and pulling and pinching and kicking ensued.

They were charged with insubordination and joining together in one cell against rules, and with *offering physical violence when apprehended*. They were sentenced to solitary confinement on Special Diet, another name for No. 1 Diet, *alias* bread and water, and were transferred at an early date.

4. FAULTY SYSTEMS

(a) *Loyalties*

(The writer has had experience, as an inmate, of both reformed and less-reformed Borstals.)

The ideal stand for a Borstal boy to make is, either to fight desperately the authority which holds him, or to accept that authority and put one's whole weight behind them. It is very hard to take up either of these stands on entering Borstal. Usually there is neutrality, a compromise. *Esprit de corps* is a plant that will not grow in the echo of three years. Cells may become rooms, and screws—housemasters, but through it all, three years remain three years. But what boy has the endurance, the pluck, the stoicism to fight, fight 'em to the bitter end of that long sentence. No! he has to compromise. So we have a curious state, where the Housemasters, with their public school code, say, 'Play the game, stop anything that is 'likely to affect the discipline of our school, Borstal.' 'Sneak and squeal and run to me, there's nothing wrong or mean in it; it is noble, you are saving them, helping us, getting yourself a Leadership, so come on, help us!'

Then the prison code leaks through: 'They are our captors, our natural enemies, fight them; if you can't fight, if you prefer the peace of neutrality, for God's sake don't blow the flute! it's treacherous! Society has put you away for a small wrong-doing, they call you an enemy of society! Well are you a traitor to your side? A Judas? sell us, for your discharge?' It amounts to that. And so we have these two sides pulling ... they will always pull, they spoil the training with which society seeks to mend these young offenders.

Give them a Borstal where they will be pulling together, it can be done! The Home Office can make a satisfactory job of these 'training camps'.

(b) *Sex*

(The first four items are extracts from a chaplain's diary, the fifth is a heavily bowdlerised extract from an account of a Borstal dormitory by an inmate.)

(i) 'Settle a problem for us', said a lad to me on Christmas night; 'Is it better to "do a teddy" or go over to N ... House?' Which being interpreted means, 'We are in urgent need of a sex outlet. Shall we then abscond in the hope of picking up a woman, or shall we go over to N ... House where, it is commonly said, are many younger lads ready to give us the gratification which we need.'

(ii) 'At the Institution Board this morning the case of a lad who was doing all in his power to be kept on here was quoted. It was said that the lad ought to be on the discharge list, but that he refused to put the necessary money in the Bank so that he might avoid discharge. The reason being, that he is so much in love with another lad that he does not wish to leave him. "What he needs", said —— of all people, "is three months in Wandsworth prison." And —— is a Quaker who genu-

120

inely believes in Love. And the lad is a simple soul who, according to his lights (which seem to me to have gleams of beauty in them) believes in love.'

(iii) 'To-night, I have found two lads in the cells—located only—for being discovered in the same bed. B... has proved himself a sane human being, and proposes to take no drastic steps. He is waiting to decide whether to separate the boys into different houses. How difficult are these things!

Here are two lads, who are desperately and genuinely in love with each other—a rare state of things in Borstal. Indecent behaviour mutual masturbation, sodomy are common enough. Love-affairs are rare. The whole essence of sex is reciprocity. Women are unobtainable. Sex cries out in these hefty young men for gratification. To find an outlet for his urge in reciprocal love—even in reciprocal lust—is surely a better healthier thing than to find it in solitary masturbation. Yet one cannot, one dare not say this.—Nevertheless it is my convinced opinion.'

(iv) A lad was heard to remark yesterday, when speaking of the difficulty of meeting, or not meeting, the demands of the sex urge in this place:

'Gawd, if they keep me here much longer, I shall be having a baby myself.'

(v) I awake to the harsh clatter of the electric bell. Some idiot walks through the dormitory, shouting, 'Come on, get out of it, you lazy bastards.' He goes over to one of the beds and strips the clothes off, revealing a boy completely nude. 'What, you on heat?', shouts the idiot. The boy on the bed laughs. A titter runs round the dormitory. The idiot picks up a slipper and swipes at the offending object. The boy on the bed who is one of the 'leery' (which means rough, crude, rude, ignorant) boys of the house begins to strut down the dormitory. This delights the rabble who encourage him with shouted remarks.

The leery boy stoops, if it is possible to stoop from this position, to ridicule. He places one hand on his hip and purses his lips, making a sucking noise. 'Ah yer lovely thing', he says in an affected manner. Then, changing his tone, he runs over to G's bed...

121

(c) *Absconding*

(Absconding, known in Borstal as 'scarpering', is a major problem at all institutions where people are confined against their will. At the newer Borstals 'scarpering' is easier. Will it, for that reason, become more frequent? The following diary extracts show some of the reasons Borstal boys have, or think they have, for 'scarpering'.)

(i) In the cells is a lad who has been discovered tampering with the lock of his door with a view to absconding. He has already absconded once. A serious view is therefore taken of his case: and he has been put on a No. 2 Diet. 'He broke his promise to me,' B... complains, 'He gave me his word not to attempt to abscond again.' An attempt, and usually a successful attempt, is always made to extort this promise from an absconder. This is the technique. The boy is shut up in the cells and is led to believe that, if he promises never to abscond again, his time 'down below' will be short. He promises. When later on he breaks this ridiculous, immorally extorted promise the aggrieved Governor, or Housemaster, as the case may be, looks upon him with sorrow and anger, and says, 'You have let me down.' Thus the unhappy lad is had both ways. The plight of this lad in question had been exacerbated by the fact that the night officer had, ever since his first attempt at escape, switched on the light in his locked room, and peered in through the spy hole several times every night. 'It maddened me so', said the lad, 'that I determined to have another go.'

(ii) A... was very interesting on the psychology of absconding. He said that lads here again and again abscond, not with any real hope of getting away, but because at intervals fits of depression come upon them (fits of being 'browned off') for a dozen reasons, and the vista of the months stretching ahead of them seems quite interminable, and they feel they must do something to let themselves go. 'Breaking all the windows in the Institution', he said, 'would answer the same purpose. But they don't do that. They scarper.' He was insistent that more liberty, more days out, would make the running of the place much easier. He was sceptical of the training here. He acknowledged

122

that, thanks to J . . . he had made progress in his music and learnt something about carpentry.

(iii) K. is meditating an abscond again. I think I dissuaded him.

'It's all the same here day after day, the same', he said. 'I can't stick it.'

'Oh dear,' said I, 'I wish I were Governor and could give you a day off now and then to go where you liked.'

'A day,' he said, 'two hours would be enough. None of us would scarper if we could have two hours away on our own every now and then.' K. knows. He is seventeen.

(d) *Unsuitable Cases.*

(The more attention shifts from mass punishment to individual treatment and cures, the more desirable will it be to separate off different characters, cases, and offences into institutions where the machinery is available for handling them. Eight Borstal Institutions have been opened since 1908, each catering for a different type of offender. Investigation and classification is carried out at Wormwood Scrubs, and cases investigated, in the words of the Borstal Association Report, 'by experts, official and unofficial, and of both sexes'. The following incidents from an official diary illustrate the acknowledged fact that the system is not yet perfect.)

(i) Bob has absconded, for the second time. He is a mental case who has more than once made attemps at suicide. I reported on him a year ago as unfit for Borstal training, for we have no machinery here to deal with him. This evening we heard news of his arrest after he had set fire to several haystacks, the crime for which he was sent to Borstal.[1]

(ii) Talked with the boy who is in here for deserting from the army and shooting up policemen. He still declares that he is obsessed with a desire to kill people, or rather to put bullets into them. This desire first came to birth in him when at rifle practice one day he hit his target—which was human shaped—and sent it toppling over. That image has dwelt in his mind.

[1] This boy was later sent to a mental home.

Yet he has shot rabbits and hated doing so. It is only the human figure which he loves to see topple over.

(iii) Talked with M . . ., who has done twenty-one months of his sentence which was the result of two convictions for indecent assault on little girls. And by way of curing the unhappy fellow of this horrible disease from which he suffers, he has been sentenced to reside in an establishment which exists for the cure and punishment of thieves. And has been given to B . . . for treatment. I failed utterly to help him in any way. 'I am sick and tired', he said, 'of being interviewed, cross examined. I don't want any more of it.' I apologised for asking him to talk of himself. I did not, as a fact, know the reason for his conviction until he volunteered the information. After which I did try to find out from him why he had done what he did. But it was useless. I appeared merely as an inquisitive inquisitor in his eyes. 'God pulls me one way, the devil another', was all his comment.

(9 days later)

I had a further interview with Matthew, at his own request. He is a poor friendless bewildered creature, at a complete loss to understand how incarceration with burglars and thieves can cure him of his horrible craze for indecently assaulting little girls, a crime for which Lady B . . . advocates the 'cat'. He has been here twenty months. The only help which he has received ever since his first arrest has taken the form of lectures on the enormity of his crime, exhortations to 'purity' of living in the future. Yet all he has wanted has been a little help in disentangling his sorely tangled mind. He has been religiously brought up, and is a Communicant here. He dreams repeatedly of bulls chasing him. The religious training he has received has planted in his mind a horror of the sinfulness of sex.

(iv) Interviewed a lad who is leaving after twenty-six months here, which he has done as punishment for indecent assault on a girl of eighteen. During all that time no one has attempted to do anything for him in any way different from what is done for the young, light-fingered gentlemen with whom he has consorted for the last two years. His case is more difficult than

M . . . And he is more difficult to help, for he is an agricultural labourer of low intelligence. He has had rows at home, is (or was) very violent tempered (he 'assaulted' the police when the arrested him), has never had sexual connection with a woman, and has been perpetually obsessed with the thought of the delight of such a connection. He has often taken girls out, and kept company with them, but they were 'nice girls', and it would have been wrong to have sex relations with them. So he let his mind dwell on thoughts of the forbidden pleasure, till it became too strong for him. He attempted to get what he wanted on two occasions (one undiscovered) with solitary girls on a dark road at night. I think I did something for him by persuading him that sex was a 'nice' thing, and that he might in future look for a 'nice' girl to share that 'nice' thing with him. No one up to date has ever done anything for him, except lecture him from the altitude of the pure-living man. The pathos of it all. I suppose if he had been a few years older he would have received the 'cat'.

(v) Saw C . . . who is going out to-morrow. An interesting case of schizophrenia. An arson merchant. He set fire to a big warehouse in Liverpool and watched it burn.

'It wasn't me that did it', he said, 'it was another fellow inside me, and I enjoyed watching him do it.'

He has been here for two years, and no one has attempted to treat him with any understanding or knowledge.

(vi) Spent a great part of the afternoon in the cells, mostly with S . . . He is perpetually down there for being 'unsatisfactory', 'insolent' and all the rest. He has been here for twenty-two months. He was a 'Leader', but was soon degraded to a 'Brown'. His housemaster is now saying that Wandsworth is the only thing for him. The boy is a grand, naturally cheerful, friendly Scotsman, who has been pretty badly knocked about by his father and was sent to a Reformatory at ten years old as being 'beyond parental control.' Here he was several times caned. He had repeated caning at his elementary school (on the hand). He has never had any real love in his life. Four years ago he lost the sight of an eye in a motor-cycle accident. Since he has been here his eye has been removed, and he has been given a glass one. He dreams of being rich and grand, and of deeds of violence which he commits. He is a very violent tempered fellow. He feels himself, owing to his upbringing, a failure. The loss of his eye and especially the operation here, have intensified that feeling. In compensation he gives way to violent language and behaviour, and in consequence is forever being found in the cells. The more violent he becomes, the more violently he is treated. Yet he is, for anyone with an elementary knowledge of psychology, the easiest creature in the world to understand and help.

(Next day)

I visited S . . . to-night in the cells. He was also visited by M . . . and the Chief, all offering him good advice. What unscientific folly it all is, and it is repeated daily, a difficult case being messed about by half a dozen different people, most of them working on no plan at all.

(vii) The interesting history of inmate T . . . Left fatherless at the age of ten, he was placed in a home for orphans. At fifteen he was returned to his mother, and started work. Not content with his lot, he went off tramping, and was arrested as a wanderer with no fixed abode and sent to a reformatory, from where he was transferred to another reformatory, from where he absconded and was in consequence sentenced to 'three years Borstal'.

He has no criminal conviction against him and has applied for special discharge. He has been eighteen months here. The application was turned down by the Visiting Committee, as the housemaster said that he was not 'fit to go out'. The application is to be reconsidered to-morrow. Meanwhile the lad has lost his 'Blue' for slackness at labour. His housemaster, who now admits that he can do nothing for him, nor will do anything, still says that he cannot recommend him for discharge. No one seems yet to have attempted to get at the cause underlying the lad's 'unsatisfactory' state of mind. Yet it is in reality simplicity itself. According to the boy's account, which is doubtless exaggerated, he was flogged most days at the orphans' home, some thirty times at the first reformatory and half a dozen times at the last.

The result is that his unconscious reaction to every order given him is, 'Oh, you go to Hell'. This, coupled with a deep grievance at finding himself, with no criminal charge against him, in Borstal, has produced a permanent state of rebellious depression in him. 'I don't know what is the matter', he keeps on saying. 'I can't help it. I have let my housemaster down.'

It is sheer stupidity to keep him here any longer, at the mercy of officers who shout, 'Get on with your work. I'll report you to the Governor', and know no other method of treating him.

XII

HAIRCUT

'WHY don't you get your hair cut?' asked a Juvenile Court magistrate of a fourteen-year-old Army cadet. 'It makes you blind in one eye, and you spend all your time shaking your head about. It makes you look like a pansy.' The boy had pleaded guilty to helping to steal six hundredweight of lead from a bombed house. He was placed on probation for a year, and ordered to pay forty shillings costs.

'He's a lonely boy at home. He looks after his mother like a woman', said his grandmother of a thirteen-year-old East-ender. He has done a series of jobs with another lad, breaking and entering factories, and had stolen goods worth £61. 'You're a shocker', the magistrate told him. 'You are going to an Approved School for at least three years. We cannot let a fellow like you loose in London or you will be breaking into all the factories.

From *The Daily Mirror*, 18th February 1947:

BREAK THE ROD TO SAVE THE CHILD

Mr. Justice Wrottesley, at Hereford Assizes yesterday, after hearing a detective say he was unaware that a father had broken a stick over his son's back, commented:

'*There should be more breaking of sticks over boys' backs. Perhaps they would then behave better.*'

The Judge sent..., seventeen, to a Borstal Institution for three years for setting fire to a haystack on his father's farm, destroying £166 worth of hay.

Of 3,367 boys discharged from Borstal during the years 1935-38, 1,389 had been re-convicted by September 1946—41 per cent.

At the outbreak of war all Borstal boys who served not less than six months of their time were released. Of 2,817 released in 1939, 1,419 had been re-convicted by September 1946—50 per cent.

The figures are particularly striking in view of the temptations of blackout and wartime relaxations of discipline which faced the 'premature' discharges of 1939. Of the girls, 54 per cent of those discharged in 1937-38 were re-convicted by December 1943, 56 per cent of those discharged in 1939.

The number of Borstal releases in 1939 was more than three times as great as the normal figure, which suggests that about two-thirds had not served their full term. Many, since three years is a usual sentence, had served only a small fraction of it. Yet the proportion who came again before the courts was little higher the two preceding 'normal' years.[1]

In conversation with Mass-Observation, a child psychiatrist expressed the informal, and perhaps deliberately overstated, view that of those sentenced to Borstal treatment about half would remain virtually unchanged by it, and most of the rest could be treated much more simply and quickly by other means.

On the other hand, a high ranking official who had devoted his life to the study of juvenile delinquency characterised (in conversation) psychiatrists as 'nearly all introverts'. He told the story of the psychiatrist whose patient was continually making the gesture of brushing crumbs from his coat. After several sessions during which no comment had been made to the patient, the psychiatrist was seen to be brushing imaginary objects off his own coat. The patient asked what he was doing and the reply was: 'I wish you wouldn't brush your crumbs over me!' The implications of the story this officer considered 'very deep'.

There are several current signs of a new reaction against

---

[1] It is worth noticing that about half of *all* people sentenced to prison in a year have been there before, and nearly one in four are serving at least their sixth term.

psychiatric treatment at widely different levels. Thus the *Sunday Express* (30th March 1947) features an article by a Captain Rippon entitled 'Is Psychiatry Just "Plain Hooey"?', in which the proposal to substitute 'corrective establishments' under psychiatrists for the old army glasshouse is ridiculed. Says Captain Rippon:

'There may be a case of a warrior who has entered the maw of a psychiatrist emerging therefrom, but I have never heard of one.'

And Clive Bell, in 'My View of Art' (*Grand Perspective,* Contact Books, 1947):

'Fortunately, pushed to its logical conclusion and made to explain everything, the Freudian hypothesis yields such deliriously comic results that it is unlikely ever to be generally accepted.'

Outside psychiatry, when disciplinary training fails, old-fashioned common-sense and kindliness may be tried. A youth of eighteen, inmate of a Borstal or Approved School for four years except for periods of absconding, pleaded guilty to factory breaking and asked for twenty other housebreaking and shopbreaking offences to be taken into consideration. The Prison Commissioners recommended further Borstal treatment. But the firm which had previously employed him was willing to offer him his job back. In binding the offender over the Judge remarked:

'You are a very remarkable example of the utter and complete futility of Institutional treatment. I am sorry to say that I most profoundly disagree with the Prison commissioners. Their treatment up to date has been a complete and utter failure.'

It is, indeed, abundantly clear in our material that in very many cases nothing which happens to the young delinquent during his (often lengthy) stay at institutions has a perceptible effect on his delinquent habits after his release.

The effects of removing the opportunity for Bill—with whom we started this report—to express the symptoms of his sexual illness were no worse and no better than the probable effects of a haircut on a small-time thief.

Like Bill, the thief would remain the same, nursing his

130

desire to steal as Bill nursed his desire to rape and hurt. The desire might not be overwhelmingly strong. The boy might steal for no deeper reason than that life seemed dull, and legitimate means of brightening it hard to find. Like the boy of psychiatric case histories, he might go thieving symbolically—stealing the love that no one would give him as a child. He might steal in desperation, to help sick parents or a young wife for whom he was unable adequately to provide. He might steal for a hundred and one reasons, and most probably he would be at best only dimly aware of them. If his early thefts were slight, and he started young, it might be several years before his progress was complete. At his first appearance in court, maybe, the case would be dismissed. Next time, a fine. Then a period of probation. A spell at an approved school, then a Borstal, then prison. Some skip several stages in the process, and some are quite readily 'cured'. Here is one, as seen through the eyes of a fellow prisoner (not a thief) :

'I first met him in a Black Maria on our way to a dispersal point for prisoners. Age 17, Scottish, living with friends in London, worked as a page in a hotel. Parents died when he was very young.

'He was confident, boastful, and quite proud of the fact that he was going to prison. This manner of his continued until his second day. He was in the same block and on the same landing as myself, and his cell was directly opposite to mine, so I saw a lot of him.

'On the second day he changed. He was weak, homesick for his friends, and regretted his crime. He was a suspect. The police said he was loitering on a main-line station with intent to steal suitcases from the incoming trains. This, he told me, was true. He had intended to steal suitcases, and had successfully done so for six months previously. He related to me the most complex and subtle plans that he and his friends periodically carried out, usually with abundant success.

'As the weeks passed in prison he became more and more regretful of his misdemeanours. He became more natural, and was the boy he undoubtedly would have been had his parents lived. He swore he would never steal again. He meant it, and

131

I believed him then, and I'm sure at this moment he is leading a comparatively respectable life. He had a few months' sentence, part of which was remitted.'

This is an example of the deterrent effect of prison, simply and encouragingly triumphant. Same prison, same time, was the Boy who Stole Leather:

'A young lad I met in the reception block interested me from the start. He was tall, fair and good-looking—when dressed. But when he was stripped for his medical, he was transformed into an anaemic tubercular, just skin and bones. He was obviously embarrassed and self-conscious of his physical condition as his blushes confirmed. He said he had had T.B. previously and had almost recovered.

'His parents had died when he was very young, and he had been, until recently, living with relatives. He was serving a short sentence as a "suspect".

'He had been convicted before and had previously been to prison for stealing from shops. He was quite bucked at being the only "old-timer" and took much delight in telling us about prison routine. His behaviour in prison was good—so as to get the full remission, he told me.

'I asked him what he would do when he got out. "Oh, the same, what else is there to do", he replied. I argued with him, and suggested many trades to which he was suited, but he merely shrugged his shoulders and said "I'll see". The next moment he would be discussing ways and means of breaking into shops and eluding the police.

'A rather peculiar aspect of this case was the fact that he always stole, if possible, leather goods—handbags, wallets and cases, etc.

'He had been taught the leather trade at a Borstal six years previously. He was very interested in leather goods and knew a lot about their manufacture. He got, he told me, extra enjoyment and satisfaction out of stealing these types of goods.

'I suggested his finding employment in this trade and asking the advice of the Governor and of the Discharged Prisoners Aid Society. He roared with laughter and said: "What, me? Been inside twice? Don't be a fool. I had a job once, a year or two ago, and they found out I'd been in prison and gave me the sack. Anyway I'm happy here. It's not pleasant and you don't get enough to eat, but it's a roof over your head".'

A few months later he went back into society, undeterred.